AUTHENTIC TRANSCRIPTIONS WITH NOTES AND TABLATURE

BEST OF
BLACK SABBATH

Music transcriptions by Steve Gorenberg and Ron Piccione

Cover photo © Jorgen Angel / Retna

ISBN-13: 978-1-4234-2962-3

 The Richmond Organization

DISTRIBUTED BY

7777 W. BLUEMOUND RD. P.O. BOX 13819 MILWAUKEE, WI 53213

Visit Hal Leonard Online at
www.halleonard.com

from *Black Sabbath*

Black Sabbath

Words and Music by Frank Iommi, John Osbourne, William Ward and Terence Butler

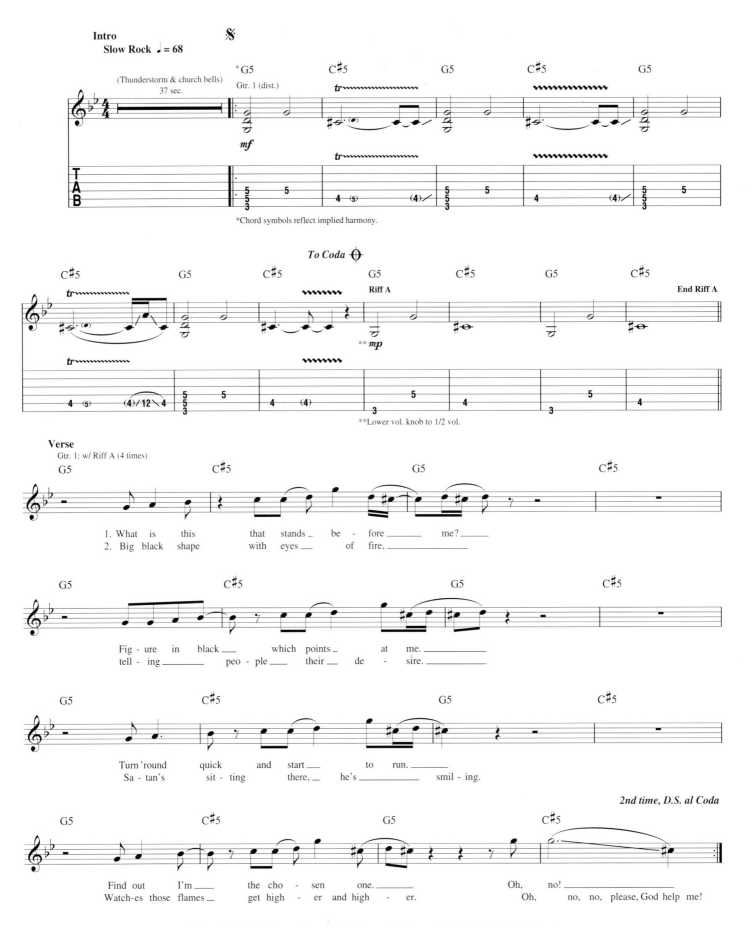

Intro
Slow Rock ♩ = 68

(Thunderstorm & church bells)
37 sec.

Gtr. 1 (dist.)

*Chord symbols reflect implied harmony.

To Coda ⊕

Riff A

End Riff A

**Lower vol. knob to 1/2 vol.

Verse
Gtr. 1: w/ Riff A (4 times)

1. What is this that stands be-fore ___ me? ___
2. Big black shape with eyes ___ of fire,

Fig-ure in black ___ which points ___ at me. ___
tell-ing ___ peo-ple ___ their ___ de-sire. ___

Turn 'round quick and start ___ to run. ___
Sa-tan's sit-ting there, ___ he's ___ smil-ing.

2nd time, D.S. al Coda

Find out I'm ___ the cho-sen one. ___ Oh, no! ___
Watch-es those flames ___ get high-er and high-er. Oh, no, no, please, God help me!

Is it the ___ end, ___ my friend? ___

Sa - tan's com - in' 'round ___ the bend. ___

Peo - ple run - nin' 'cause ___ they're scared. ___

peo - ple bet - ter go ___ and be - ware. ___ No, ___ no, ___ please, ___ no. ___

You

3

from *Heaven and Hell*

Children of the Sea

Words by Ronnie James Dio
Music by Ronnie James Dio, Terence Butler, Anthony Iommi and William Ward

Tune down 1/2 step:
(low to high) E♭-A♭-D♭-G♭-B♭-E♭

Intro
Slowly ♩ = 71

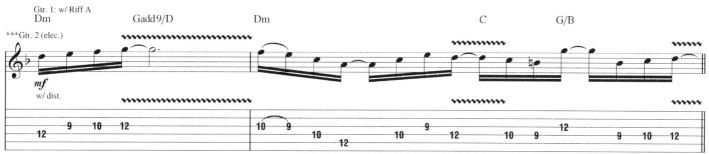

*Gtr. 1 (acous.)
*Doubled throughout
**Chord symbols reflect basic harmony.

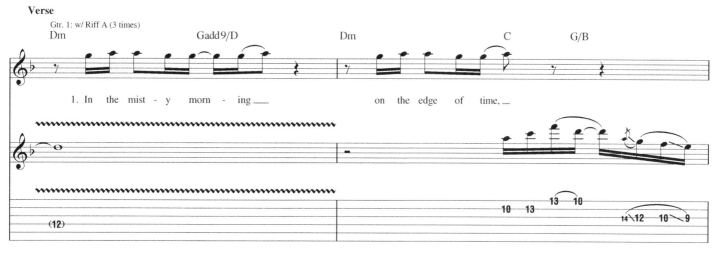

***Pickup selector set to neck pickup w/ vol. control set to 1/2 vol.

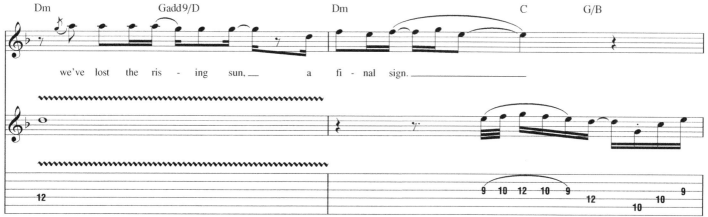

1. In the mist-y morn-ing ___ on the edge of time, ___

we've lost the ris-ing sun, ___ a fi-nal sign. ___

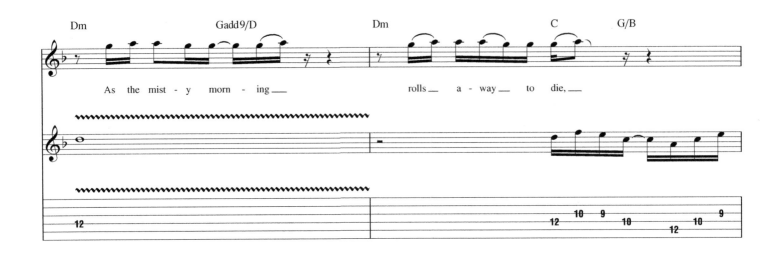

As the mist - y morn - ing _____ rolls _____ a - way _____ to die, _____

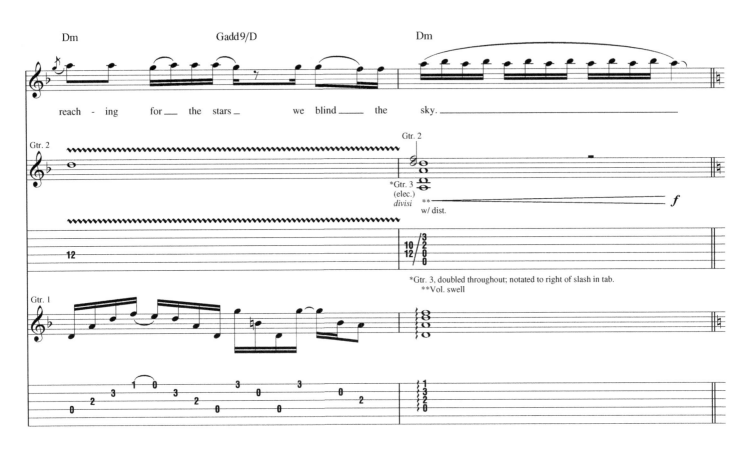

reach - ing for _____ the stars _____ we blind _____ the sky. _____

*Gtr. 3, doubled throughout; notated to right of slash in tab.
**Vol. swell

Interlude
Gtrs. 1 & 2 tacet

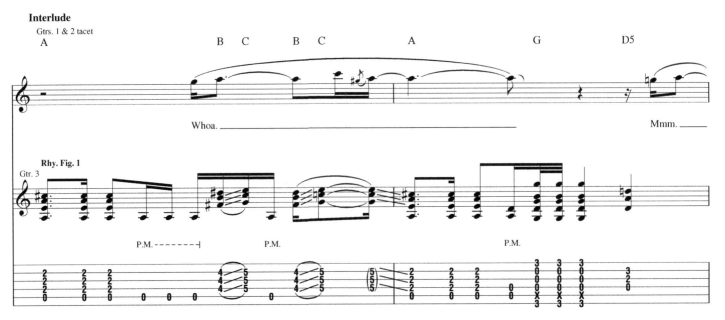

Whoa. _____ Mmm. _____

Rhy. Fig. 1

End Rhy. Fig. 1

Verse

Gtr. 3: w/ Rhy. Fig. 1 (2 times)

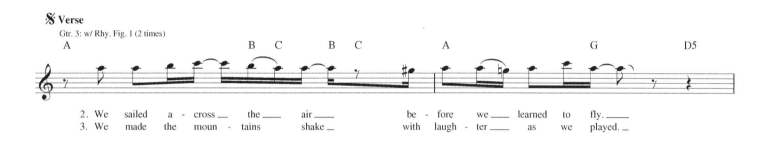

2. We sailed a - cross __ the __ air __ be - fore we __ learned to fly. __
3. We made the moun - tains shake __ with laugh - ter __ as we played. __

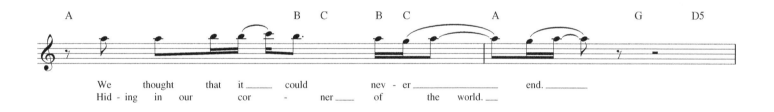

We thought that it __ could nev - er __ end. __
Hid - ing in our cor - ner __ of the world. __

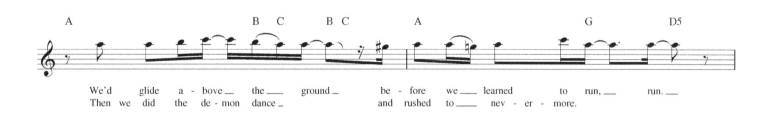

We'd glide a - bove __ the __ ground __ be - fore we __ learned to run, __ run. __
Then we did the de - mon dance _ and rushed to __ nev - er - more. __

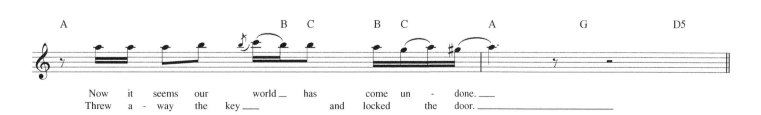

Now it seems our world __ has come un - done. __
Threw a - way the key __ and locked the door. __

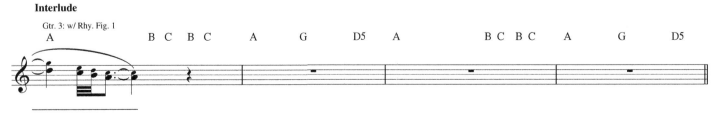

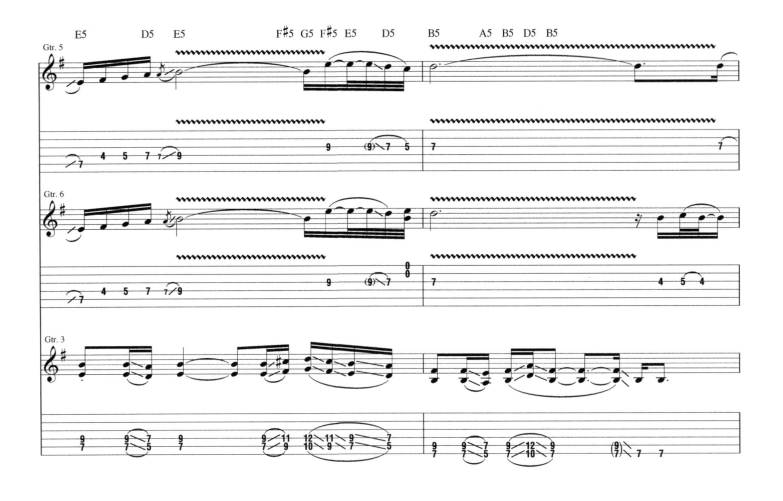

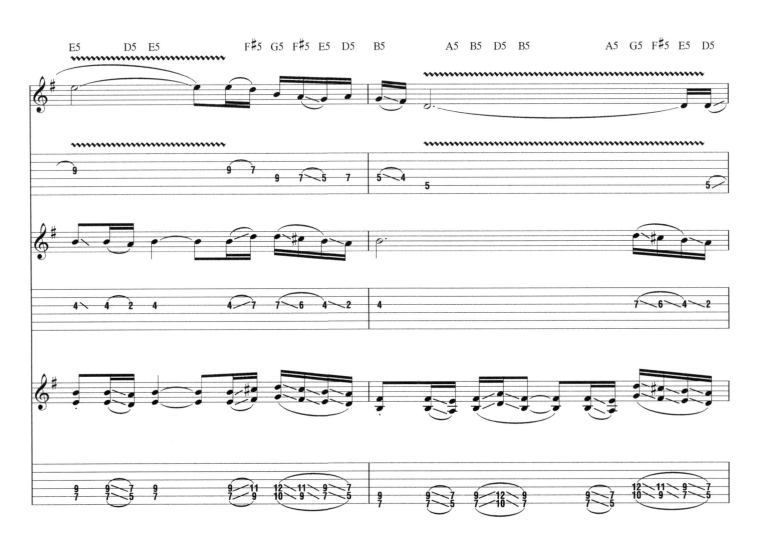

Guitar Solo

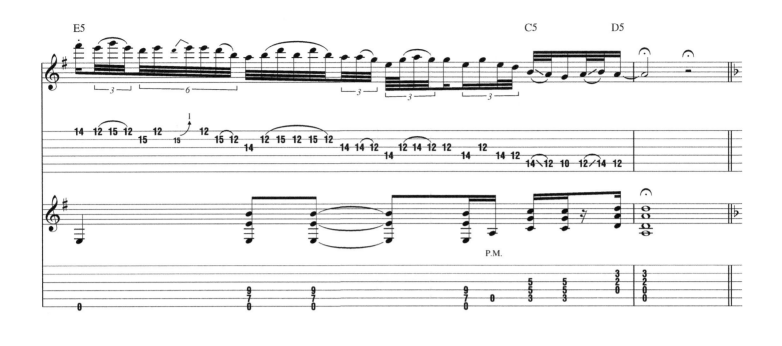

Interlude

Gtrs. 3 & 4 tacet
Gtr. 1: w/ Riff A (2 times)

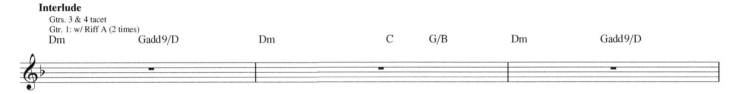

Verse

Gtr. 1: w/ Riff A (3 1/2 times)

4. In the mist - y morn - ing ____

on the edge of time, ____ we've lost the ris - ing sun, ____ the

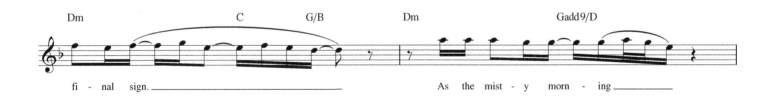

fi - nal sign. ____ As the mist - y morn - ing ____

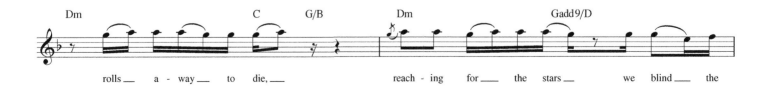

rolls ____ a - way ____ to die, ____ reach - ing for ____ the stars ____ we blind ____ the

13

from *Heaven and Hell*

Heaven and Hell

Words by Ronnie James Dio
Music by Ronnie James Dio, Terence Butler, Anthony Iommi and William Ward

Tune down 1/2 step:
(low to high) Eb-Ab-Db-Gb-Bb-Eb

Intro
Moderately slow ♩ = 90

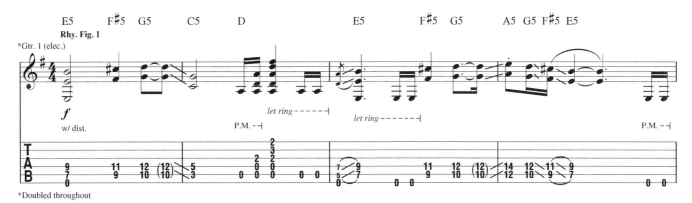

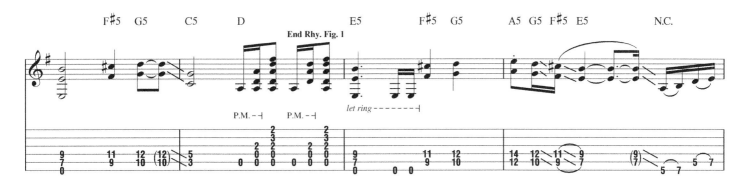

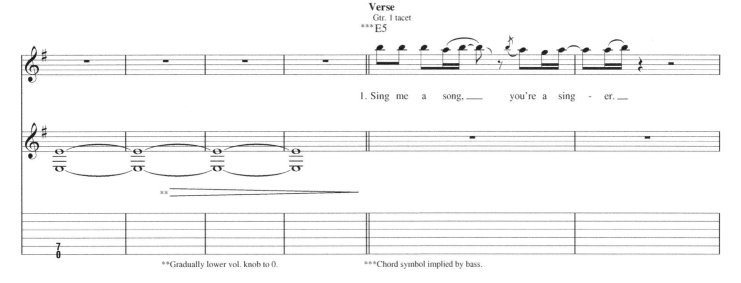

*Gradually lower vol. knob to 0.   ***Chord symbol implied by bass.

<section type="boilerplate">
TRO - © Copyright 1980 Essex Music International, Inc., New York and Niji Music, Studio City, CA
International Copyright Secured
All Rights Reserved Including Public Performance For Profit
Used by Permission
</section>

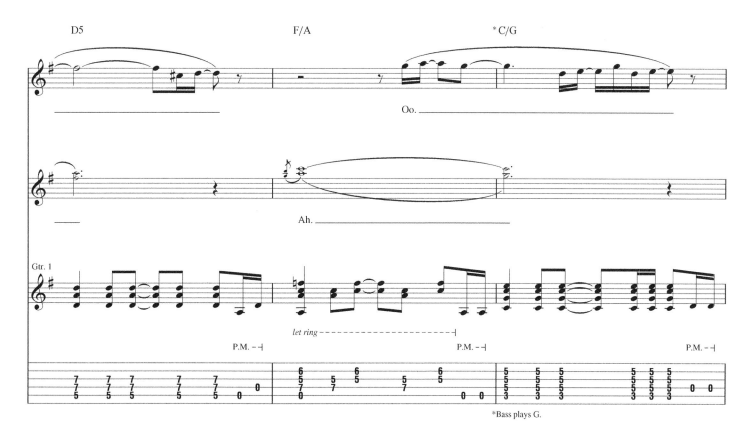

Yeah, yeah. _____

Ah.) _____

let ring - - - - - - - - - - - - ⌐ P.M. ⌐ let ring - - - - - - - - - - - - - - - ⌐ P.M. ⌐

*Bass plays B.

Interlude

Gtr. 1: w/ Riff A (2 times)

Verse

Gtr. 1: w/ Riff A (2 1/2 times)

3. Well, if it seems to be real, __ it's il - lu - sion. __ For ev - 'ry

mo - ment of truth, __ there's con - fu - sion in life. Love can be seen __ as the an -

- swer, but no - bod - y bleeds __ for the danc - er. And it's

Gtr. 1

P.M. - - - - ⌐   P.M. - - - - ⌐   P.M. - - - - ⌐   P.M. - - - - ⌐   P.M.

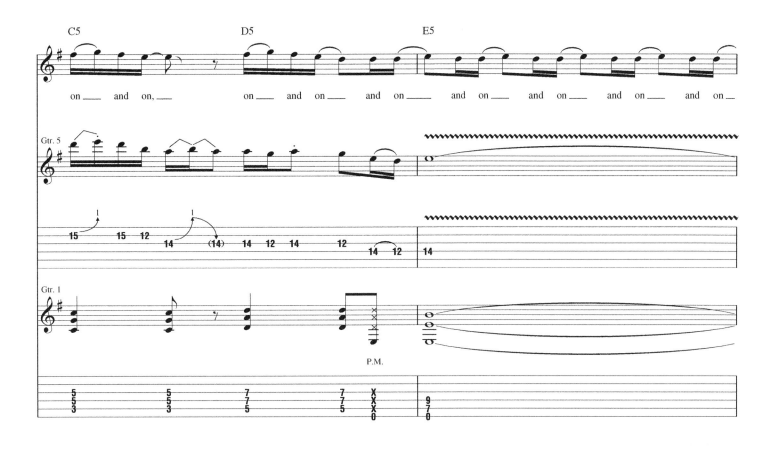

Guitar Solo

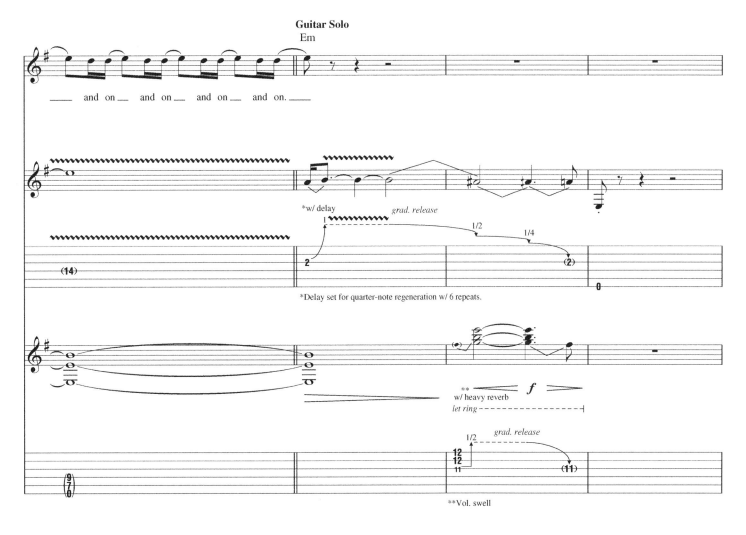

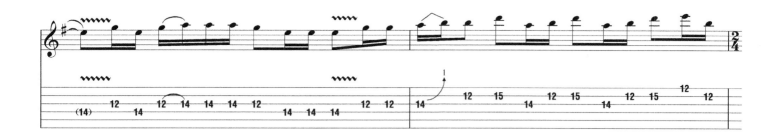

E5   G5   Am(add9)   D

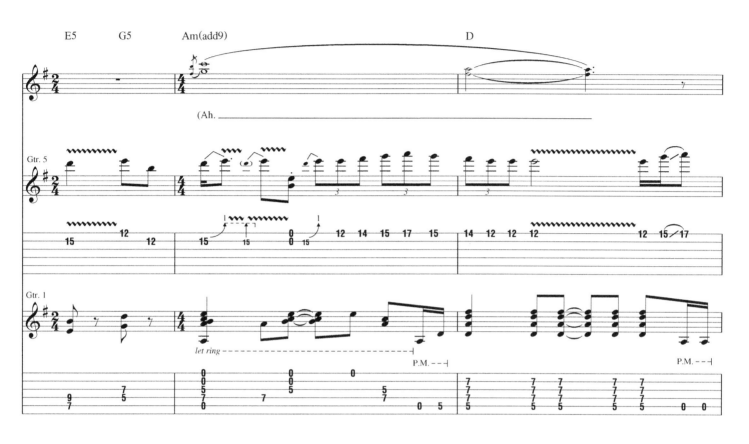

F/A   *C/G

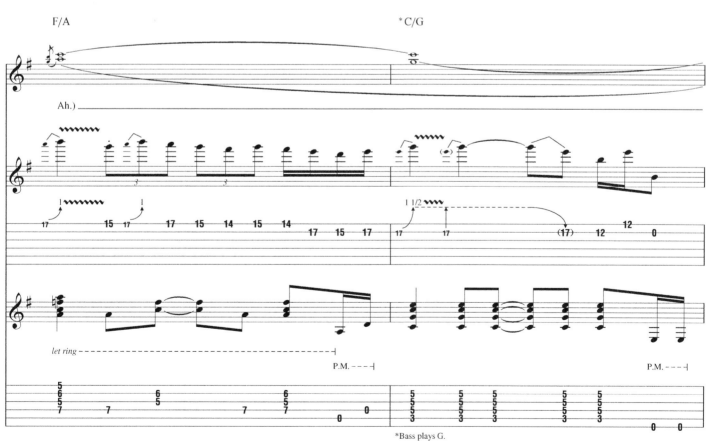

*Bass plays G.

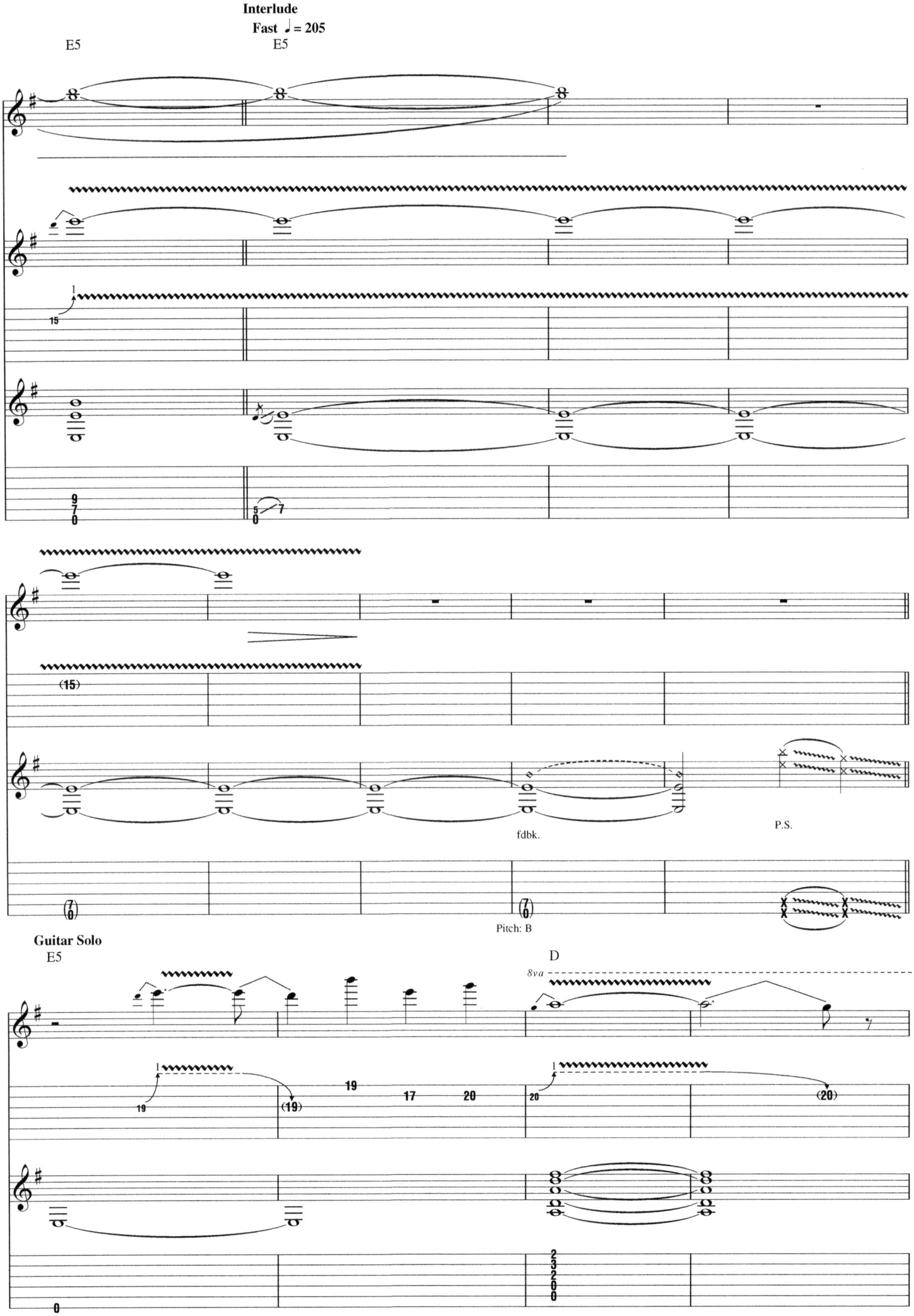
Interlude
Fast ♩ = 205
E5
E5
fdbk.
P.S.
Pitch: B
Guitar Solo
E5
D
8va

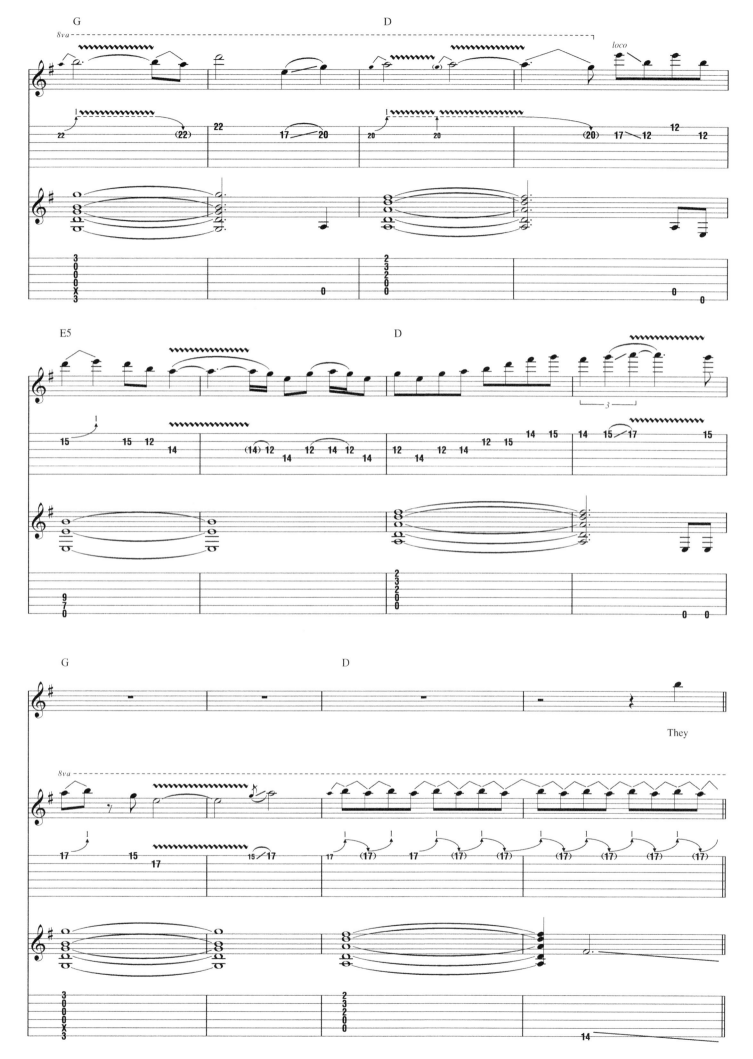

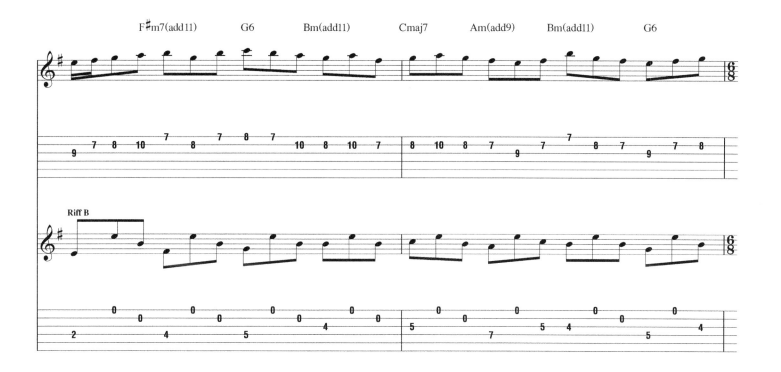

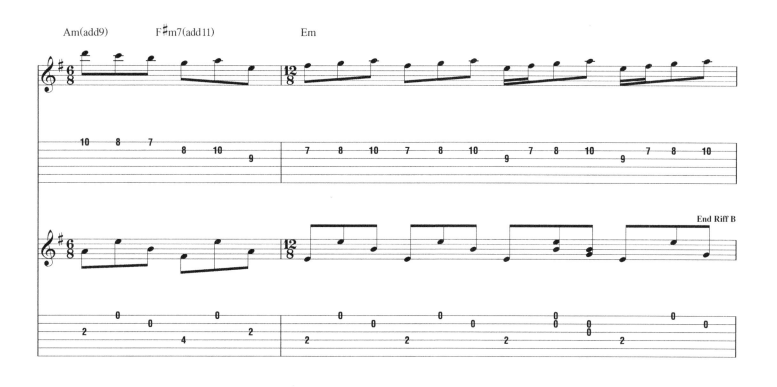

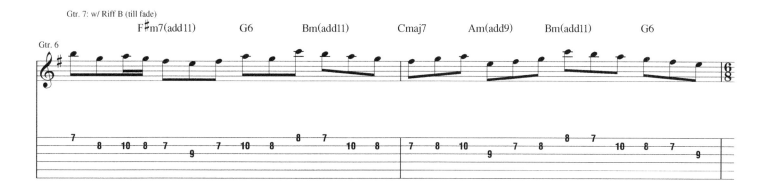

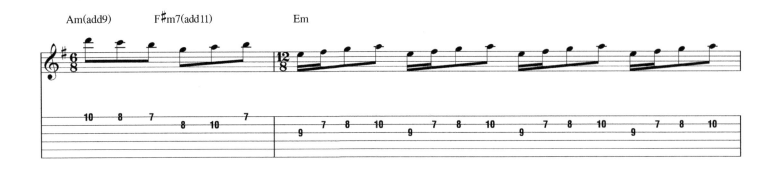

Begin fade

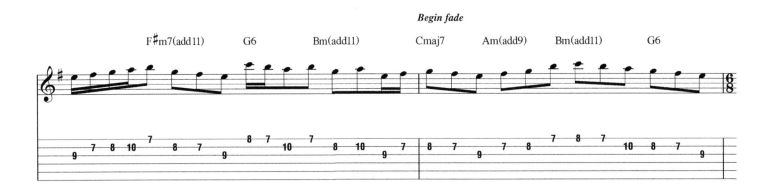

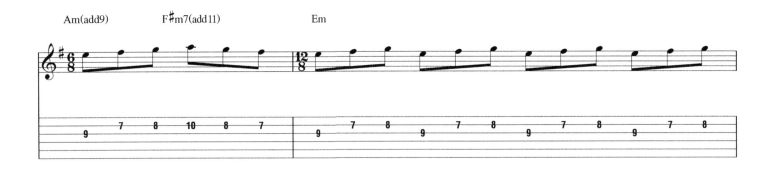

Fade out

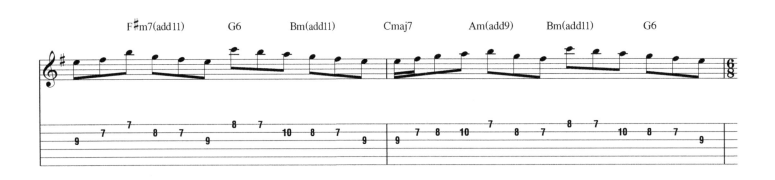

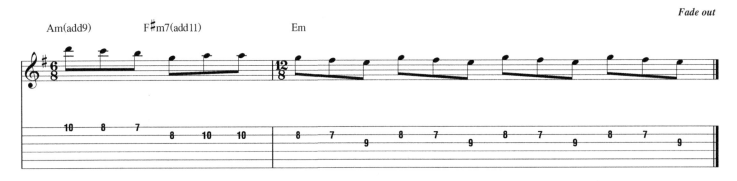

from *Sabotage*

Hole in the Sky

Words and Music by Frank Iommi, William Ward, Terence Butler and John Osbourne

Tune down 1 1/2 steps:
(low to high) C#-F#-B-E-G#-C#

*Doubled throughout

**Chord symbols reflect implied harmony.

***Set for one octave below.

𝄋 Verse

Gtr. 1: w/ Riff A (2 times)

2. I'm liv - ing in a room with - out an - y view. _____
3. I've seen the stars that dis - ap - pear in the sun. _____

I'm liv - ing free be - cause the rent's nev - er due. _____ The syn - o - nym of all the
But shoot - ing's eas - y if you've got the right gun. _____ And e - ven though I'm sit - ting

things that I've said _____ are just the rid - dles that are built in my head. _____
wait - ing for Mars, _____ I don't be - lieve there's an - y fu - ture in cause. _____

Chorus

Hole in the sky, _____

Gtr. 1
octaver off

gate - way to heav - en. _____   Win - dow in time, _____

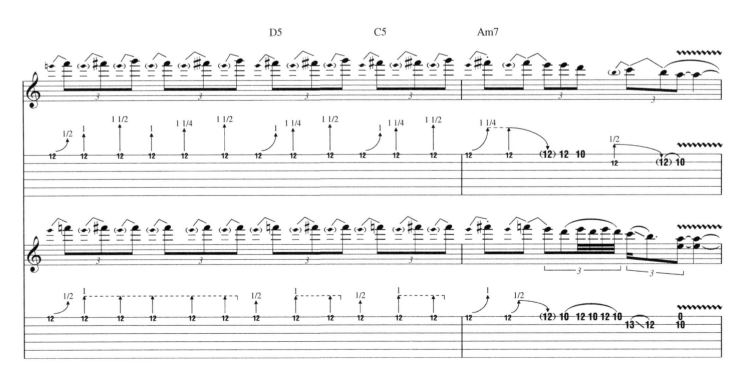

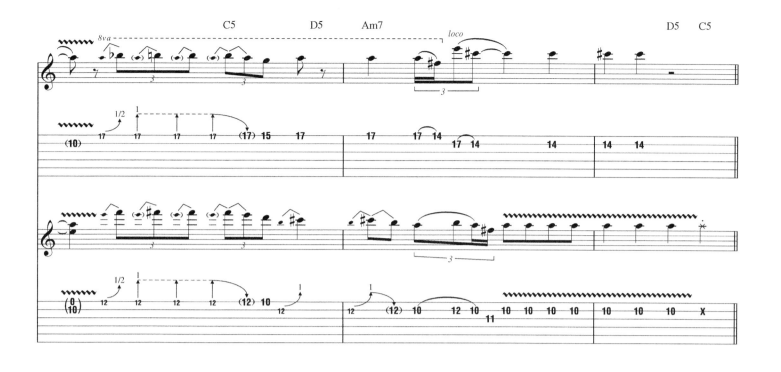

Verse

Gtr. 1: w/ Riff A (2 times)
Gtrs. 2 & 3 tacet

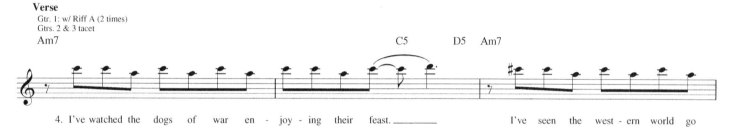

4. I've watched the dogs of war en - joy - ing their feast. _____ I've seen the west - ern world go

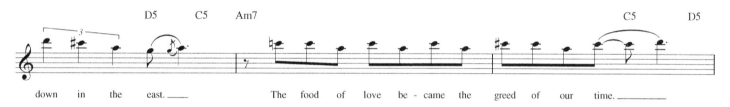

down in the east. _____ The food of love be - came the greed of our time. _____

Interlude

Gtr. 1: w/ Rhy. Fig. 1 (4 times)
Gtr. 2: w/ Riff B (4 times)

And now we're liv - ing on the prof - its of crime. _____

Outro

Gtr. 1: w/ Riff A

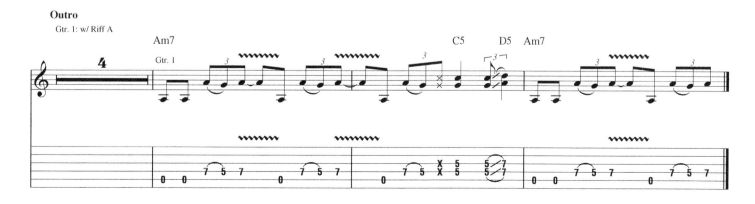

from *Master of Reality*

Into the Void

Words and Music by Frank Iommi, William Ward, John Osbourne and Terence Butler

Tune down 1 1/2 steps:
(low to high) C#-F#-B-E-G#-C#

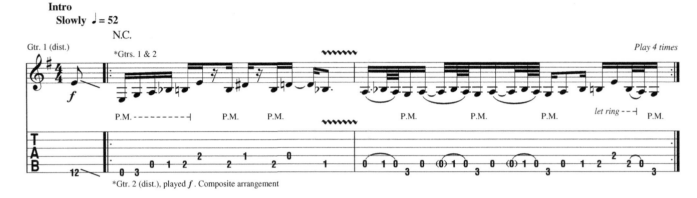

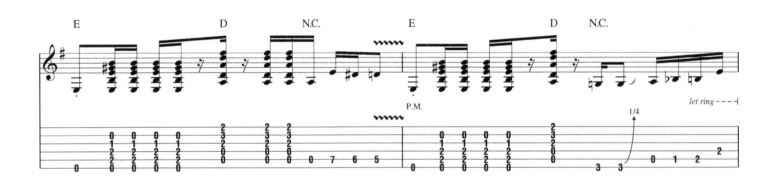

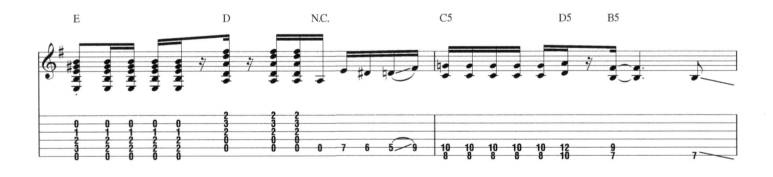

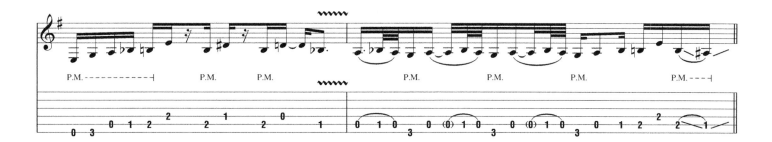

Faster ♩ = 77

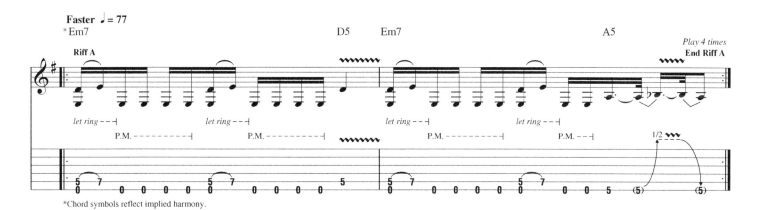

*Chord symbols reflect implied harmony.

𝄋 Verse

1. Rock - et en - gines burn - ing fuel _____ so fast, up in - to the night sky _____ they _ blast.
2. Rock - et en - gines burn - ing fuel _____ so fast, up in - to the black sky _____ so _ vast.
3. Past the stars in fields of an - cient void. Through the shields of dark - ness where _____ they _ find.

Riff B

End Riff B

let ring

let ring

let ring

let ring

P.M.

P.M.

P.M.

P.M.

1/2

**Vocs. w/ echo set for eighth-note
regeneration w/ 1 repeat throughout.

Gtrs. 1 & 2: w/ Riff B (2 times)

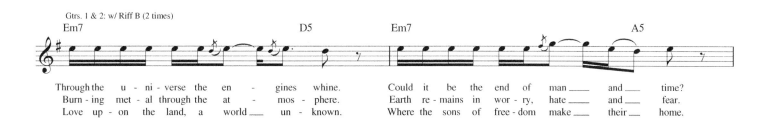

Through the u - ni - verse the en - gines whine. Could it be the end of man _____ and _____ time?
Burn - ing met - al through the at - mos - phere. Earth re - mains in wor - ry, hate _____ and _____ fear.
Love up - on the land, a world _____ un - known. Where the sons of free - dom make _____ their _____ home.

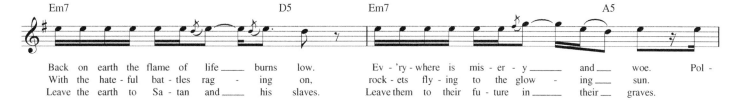

Back on earth the flame of life _____ burns low. Ev - 'ry - where is mis - er - y _____ and _____ woe. Pol -
With the hate - ful bat - tles rag - ing on, rock - ets fly - ing to the glow - ing _____ sun.
Leave the earth to Sa - tan and _____ his slaves. Leave them to their fu - ture in _____ their _____ graves.

from *Paranoid*

Iron Man

Words and Music by Frank Iommi, John Osbourne, William Ward and Terence Butler

Guitar Solo
Gtr. 2 tacet

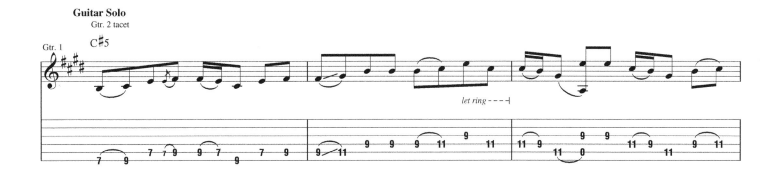

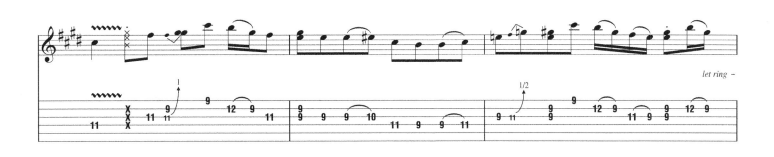

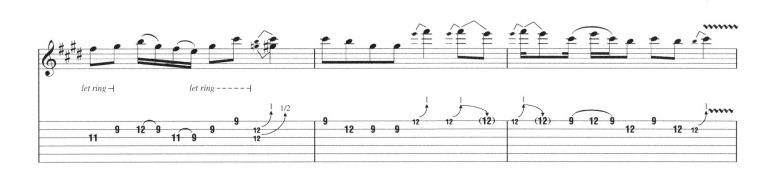

D.S. al Coda
(take 2nd ending)

Interlude
Gtrs. 1 & 2: w/ Riff C

A tempo
Gtrs. 1 & 2: w/ Riff B (2 times)

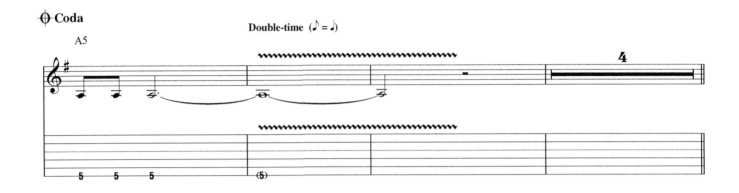

Coda

Double-time

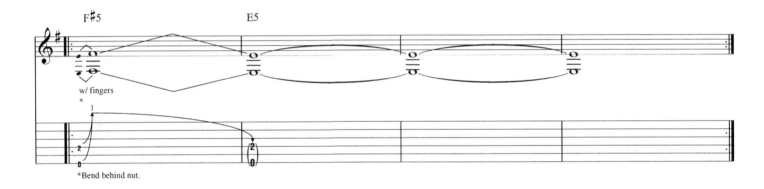

*Bend behind nut.

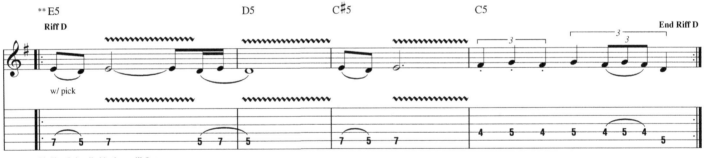

** Chords implied by bass, till Outro.

Guitar Solo

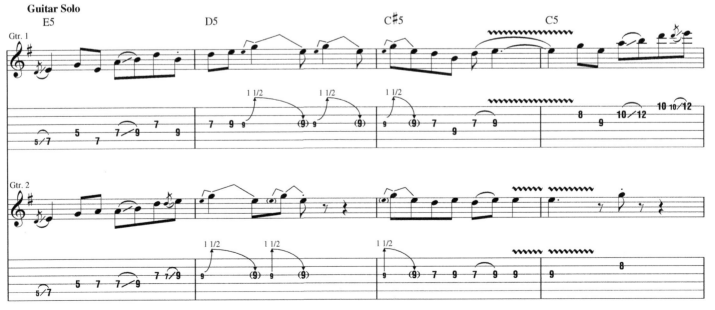

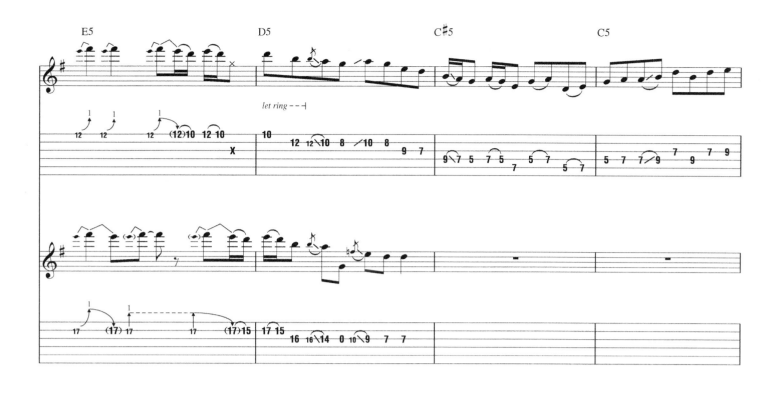

Outro

Gtrs. 1 & 2: w/ Riff D (3 times)

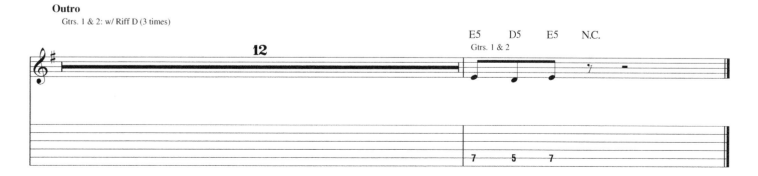

from *The Mob Rules* (remastered version)

The Mob Rules

Words by Ronnie James Dio
Music by Ronnie James Dio, Terence Butler and Anthony Iommi

1. Close the cit - y and tell the peo - ple that some-thing's com - ing to call.
2. Kill the spir - it and you'll be blind - ed, the end is al - ways the same.

Death and dark - ness are rush - ing for - ward to
Play with fire, you burn your fin - gers and

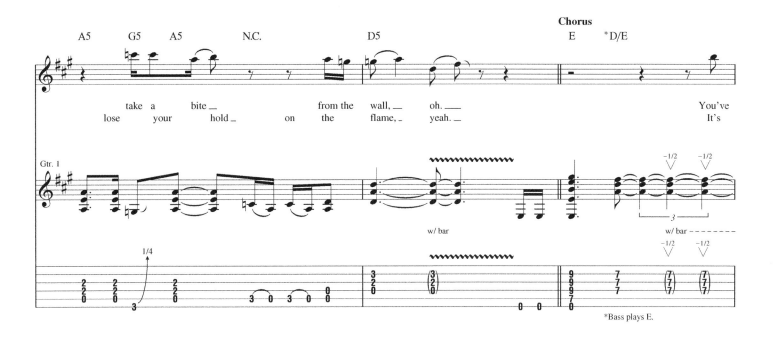

take a bite ___ from the wall, ___ oh. ___ You've
lose your hold ___ on the flame, ___ yeah. ___ It's

*Bass plays E.

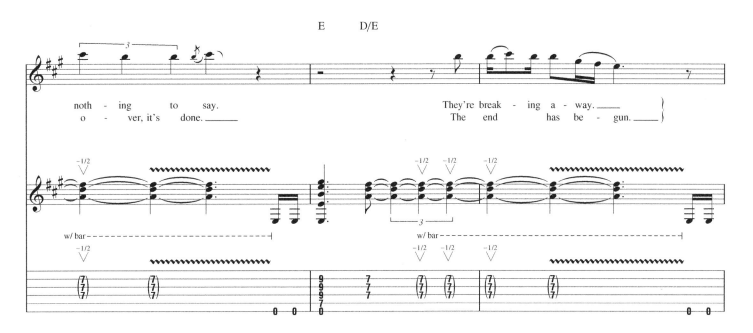

noth - ing to say. They're break - ing a - way. ___
o - ver, it's done. ___ The end has be - gun. ___

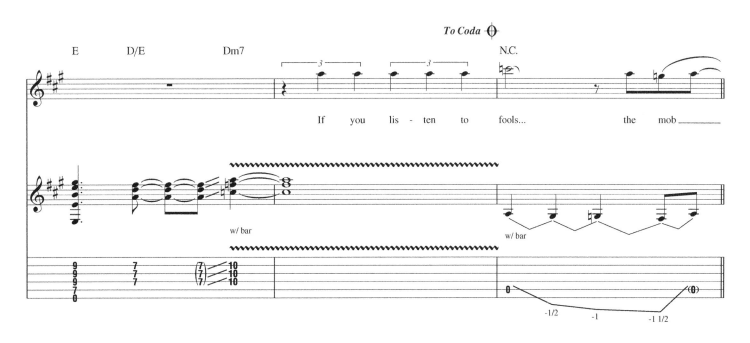

If you lis - ten to fools... the mob ___

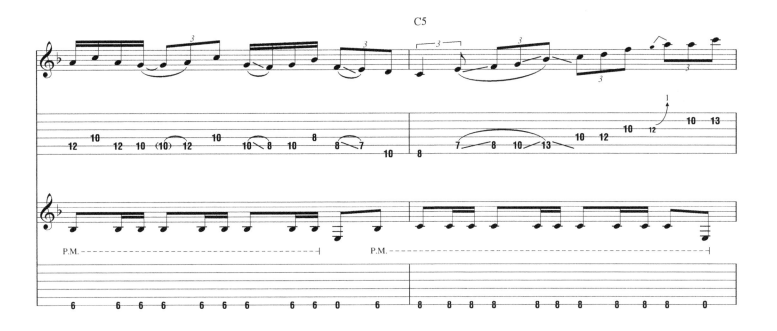

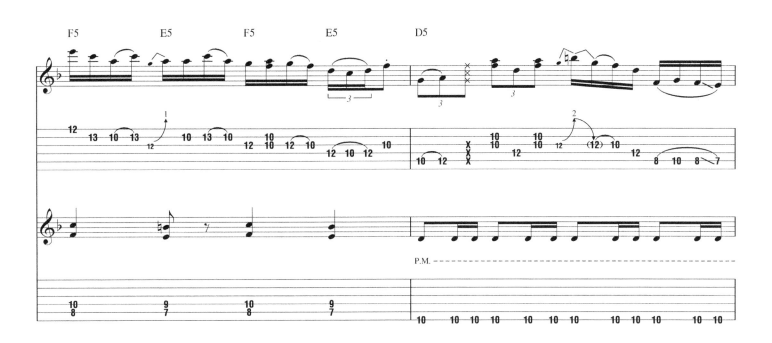

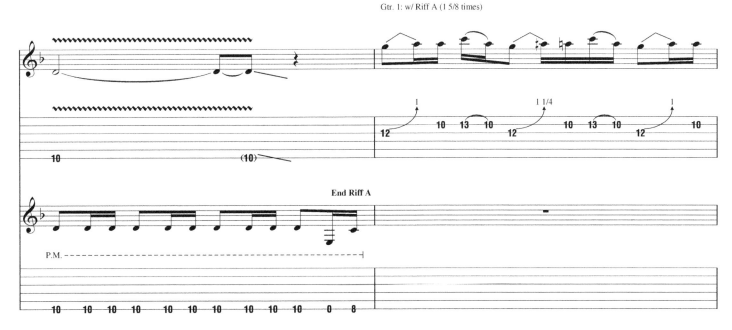

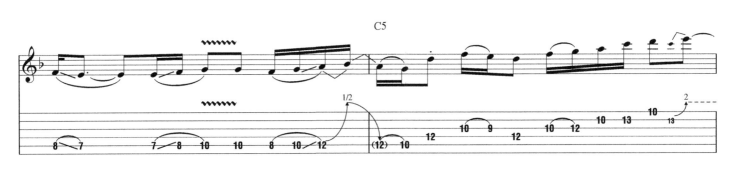

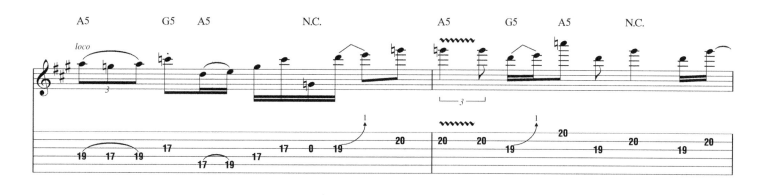

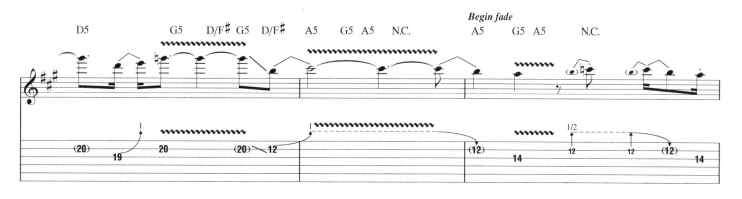

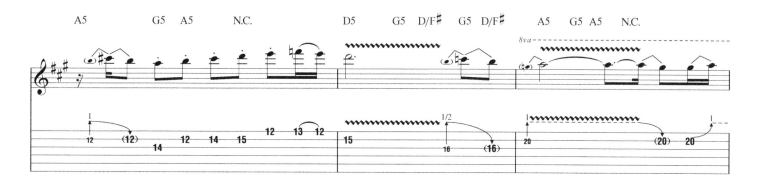

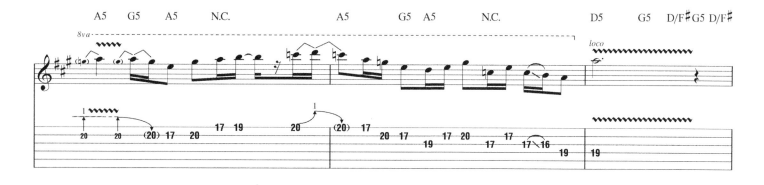

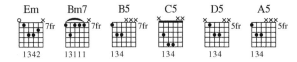

from *Heaven and Hell*

Neon Knights

Words by Ronnie James Dio

Music by Ronnie James Dio, Terence Butler, Anthony Iommi and William Ward

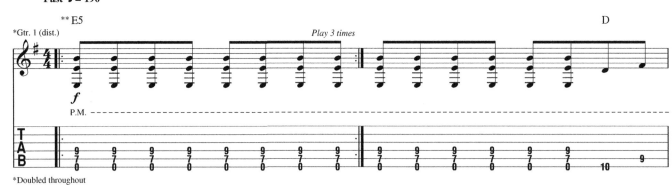

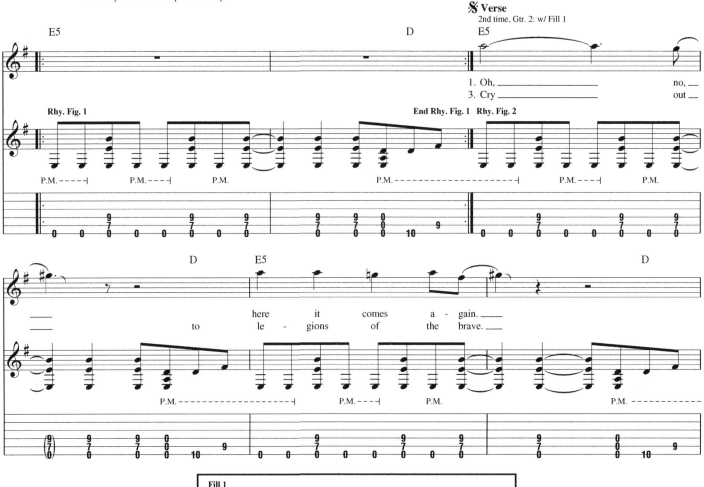

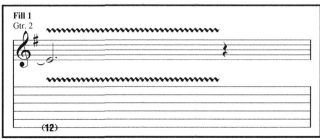

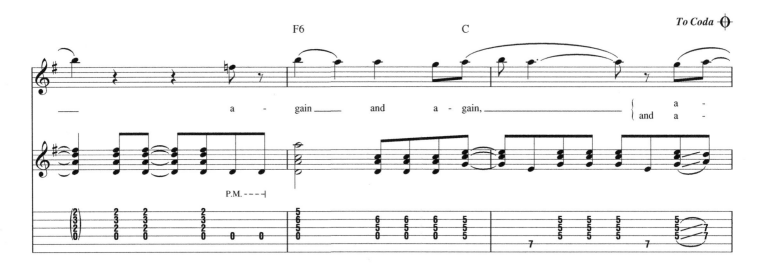

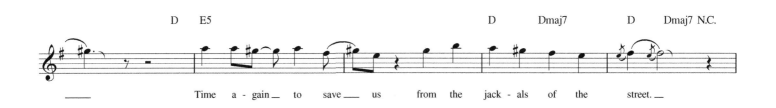

Ride ___ out, ___ pro - tec - tors of the realm. ___

Cap - tains at the helm, ___ sail ___ a - cross the sea of ___

Bridge

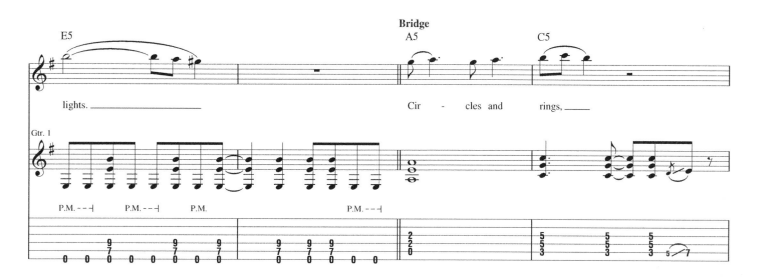

lights. ___ Cir - cles and rings, ___

Gtr. 1

P.M. ---┤   P.M. ---┤   P.M.   P.M. ---┤

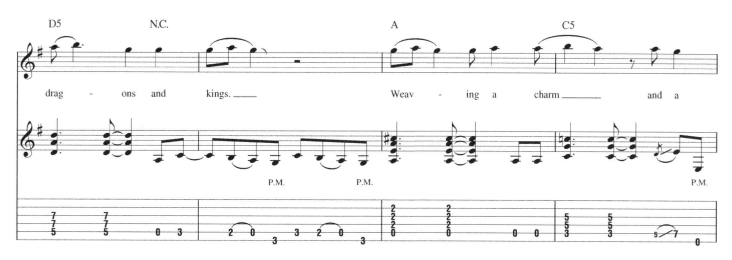

drag - ons and kings. ___ Weav - ing a charm ___ and a

P.M.   P.M.   P.M.

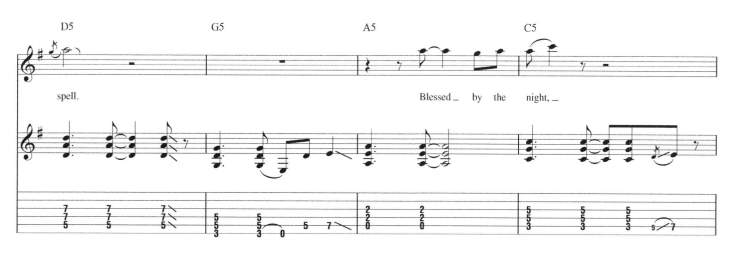

spell.   Blessed ___ by the night, ___

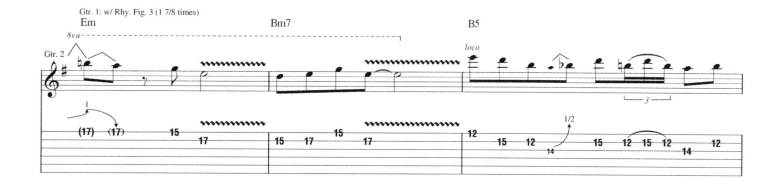

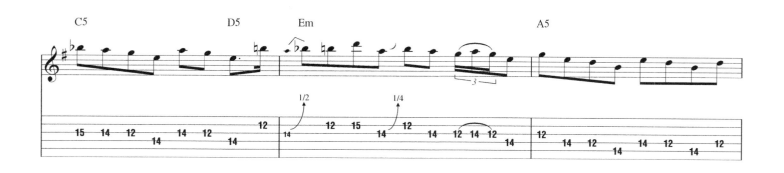

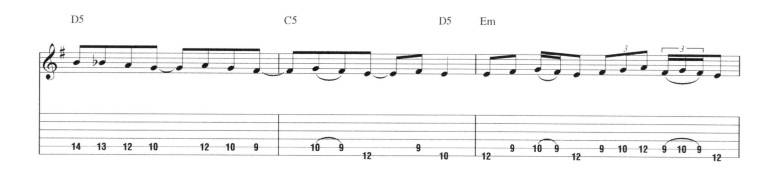

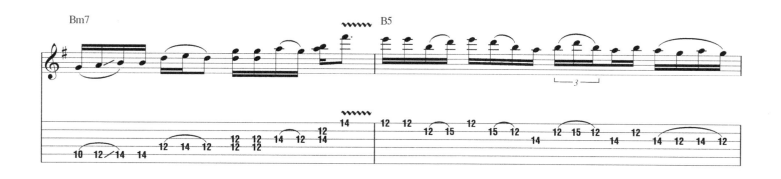

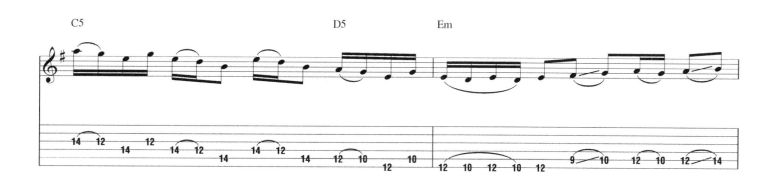

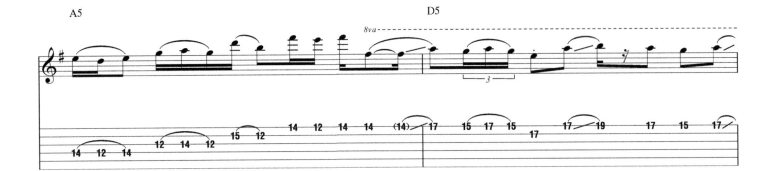

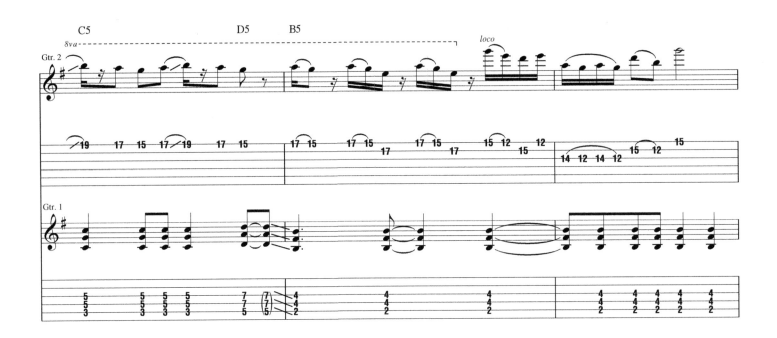

D.S. al Coda

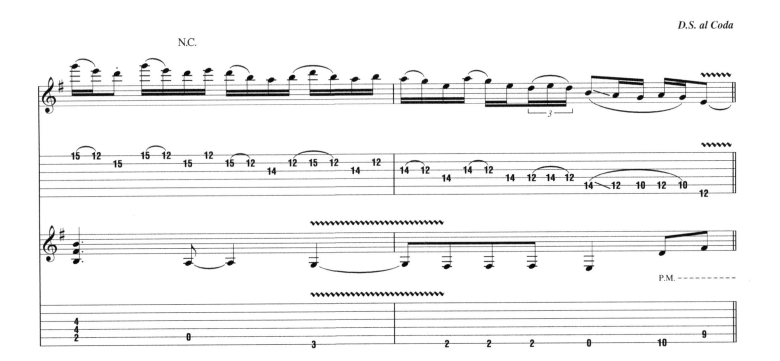

Begin fade

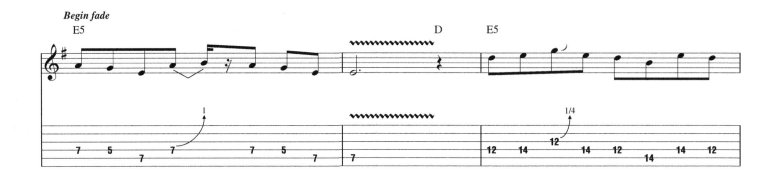

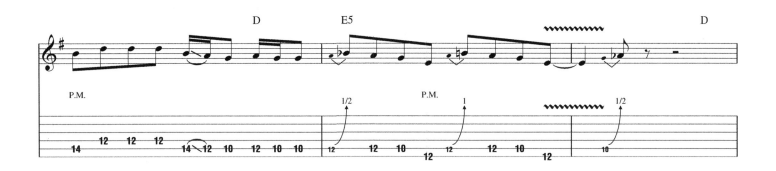

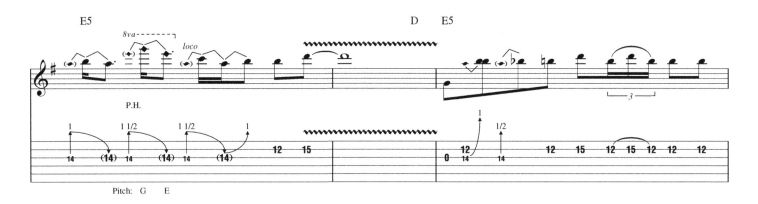

Pitch: G   E

Fade out

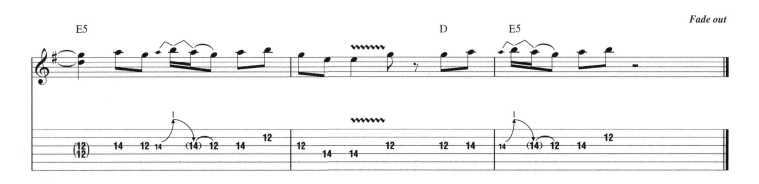

from *Black Sabbath*

N.I.B.

Words and Music by Frank Iommi, Terence Butler, William Ward and John Osbourne

*Swell to full vol.

Intro
Moderately ♩ = 104

w/ dist.

**Chord symbols reflect implied harmony.

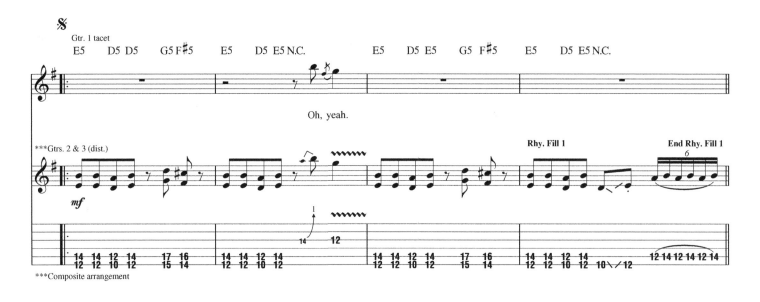

Oh, yeah.

***Gtrs. 2 & 3 (dist.)

Rhy. Fill 1

End Rhy. Fill 1

***Composite arrangement

Verse

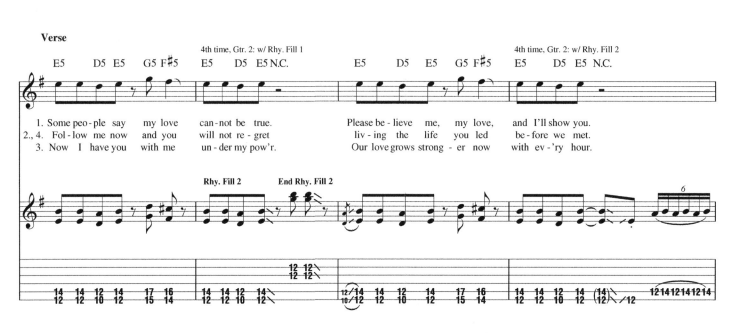

4th time, Gtr. 2: w/ Rhy. Fill 1

4th time, Gtr. 2: w/ Rhy. Fill 2

1. Some peo-ple say my love can-not be true. Please be-lieve me, my love, and I'll show you.
2., 4. Fol-low me now and you will not re-gret liv-ing the life you led be-fore we met.
3. Now I have you with me un-der my pow'r. Our love grows strong-er now with ev-'ry hour.

Rhy. Fill 2

End Rhy. Fill 2

I will give you those things you thought un-real.
You are the first to have this love of mine,
Look in-to my eyes, you'll see who I am.

The sun, the moon, the stars all bear my seal.
for-ev-er with me 'til the end of time.
My name is Lu-ci-fer, please take my hand.

Interlude

To Coda 1

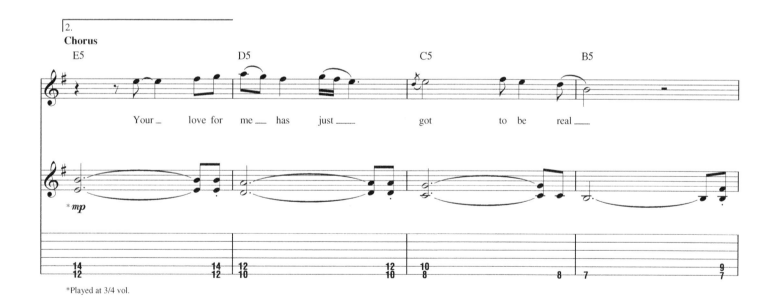

Chorus

Your love for me has just got to be real

*Played at 3/4 vol.

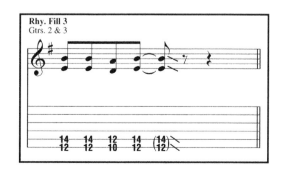

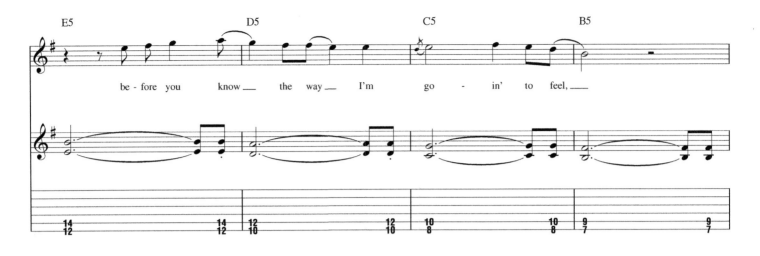

be - fore you know ___ the way ___ I'm go - in' to feel, ___

D.S. al Coda 1
(take 1st ending)

2nd time, To Coda 2

I'm go - in' to feel, ___ I'm go - in' to feel. _____

Coda 1

72

D.S. al Coda 2
(take 2nd ending)

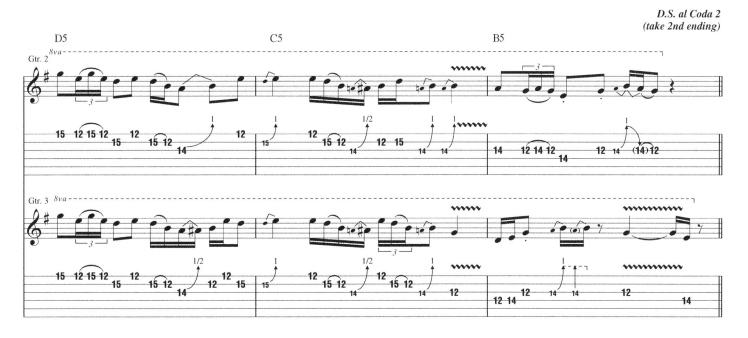

⊕ **Coda 2**

Interlude

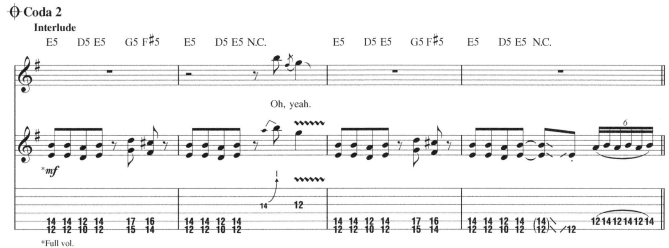

Oh, yeah.

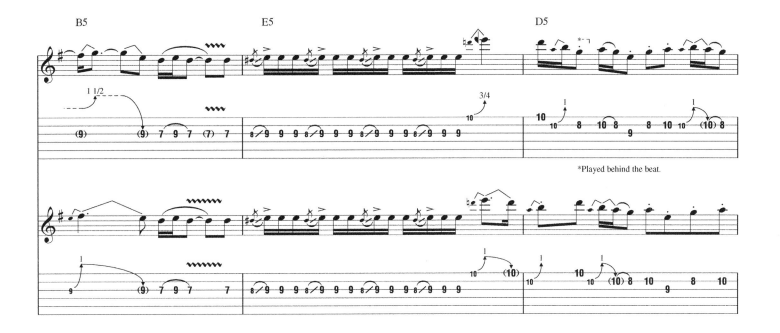

*Played behind the beat.

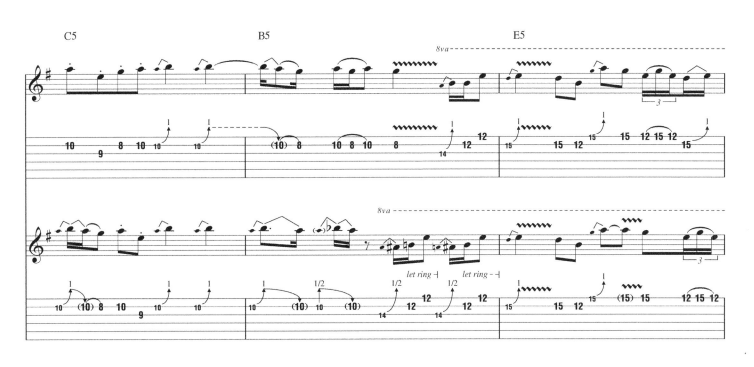

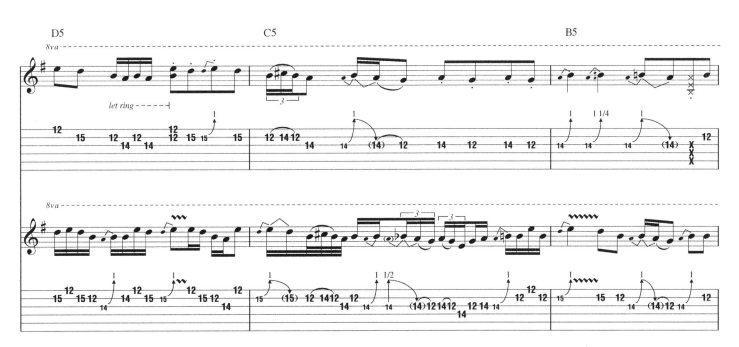

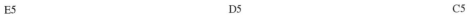

E5   D5   C5

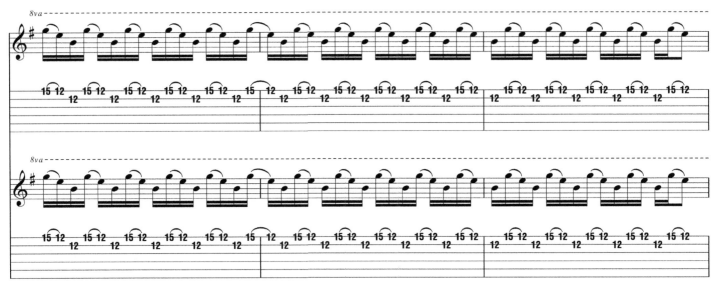

Free time

B5

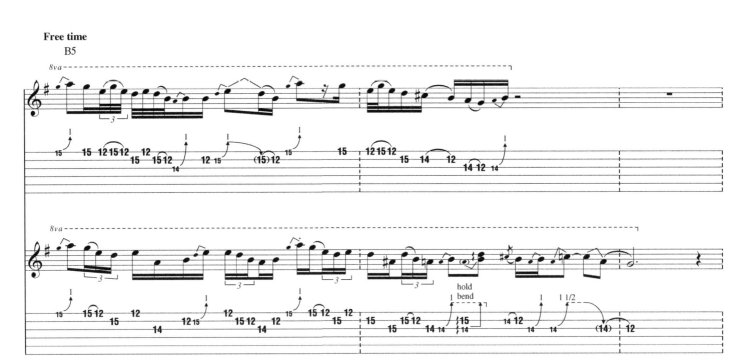

E   N.C.

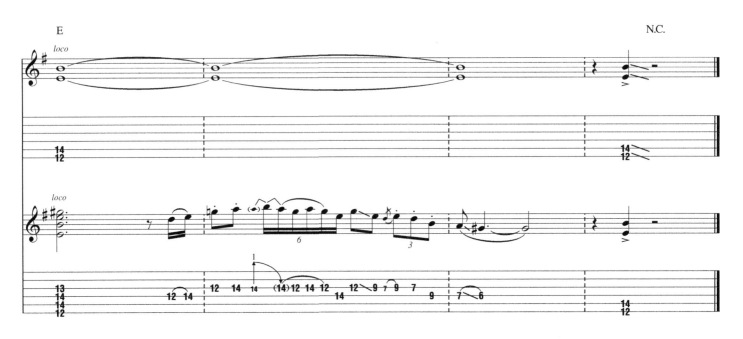

from *Paranoid*

Paranoid

Words and Music by Anthony Iommi, John Osbourne, WIlliam Ward and Terence Butler

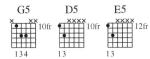

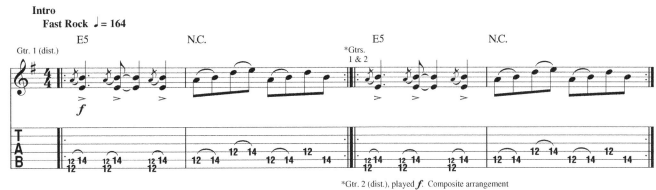

Interlude

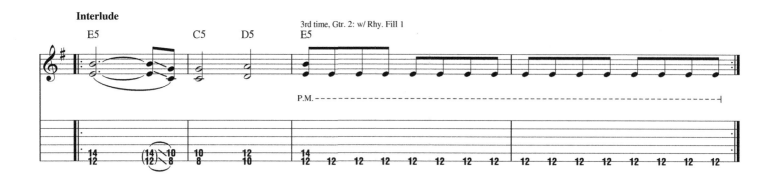

Verse

1st time, Gtrs. 1 & 2: w/ Rhy. Fig. 1
2nd time, Gtrs. 1 & 2: w/ Rhy. Fig. 1 (1st 4 meas., 2 times)

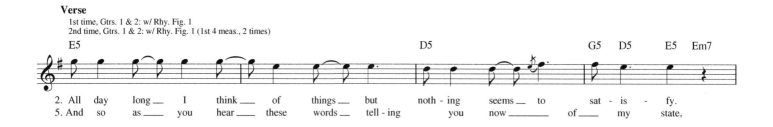

2. All day long ___ I think ___ of things ___ but noth - ing seems ___ to sat - is - fy.
5. And so as ___ you hear ___ these words tell - ing you now ___ of ___ my state,

Think I'll lose ___ my mind ___ if I ___ don't find ___ some - thing ___ to pac - i - fy.
I tell you ___ to en - joy life. ___ I ___ wish ___ I could ___ but it's too late.

Bridge

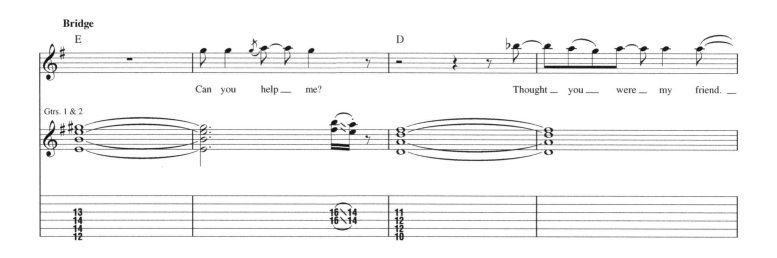

Can you help ___ me?   Thought ___ you ___ were ___ my friend. ___

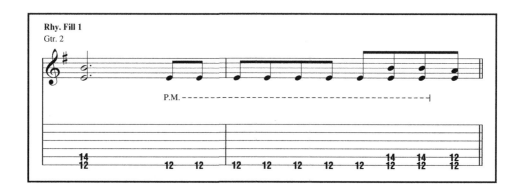

Rhy. Fill 1
Gtr. 2

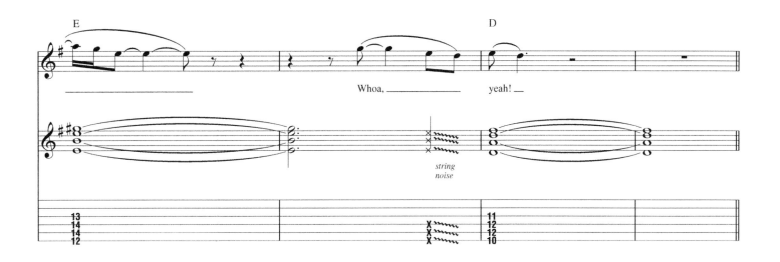

Whoa, yeah!

string noise

Interlude

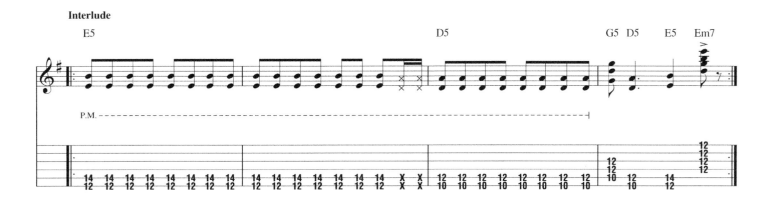

P.M. -

Verse

Gtrs. 1 & 2: w/ Rhy. Fig. 1

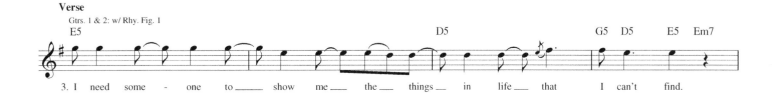

3. I need some - one to show me the things in life that I can't find.

I can't see the things that make true hap - pi - ness, I must be blind.

Guitar Solo

Gtrs. 1 & 2: w/ Rhy. Fig. 1 (1st 4 meas., 4 times)

*Gtr. 3 (dist.)

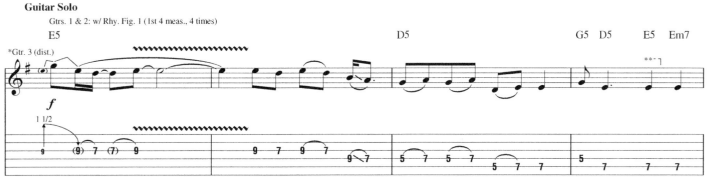

*With heavily distorted ring modulation effect in right channel.

**Played ahead
of the beat.

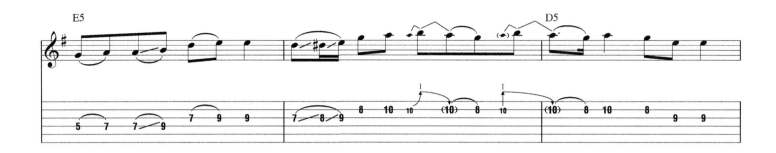

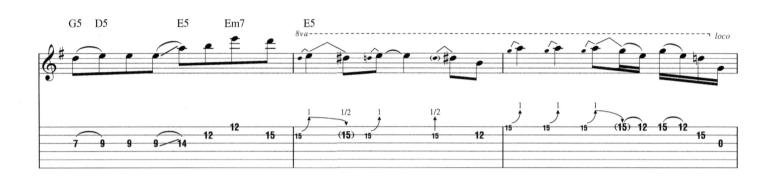

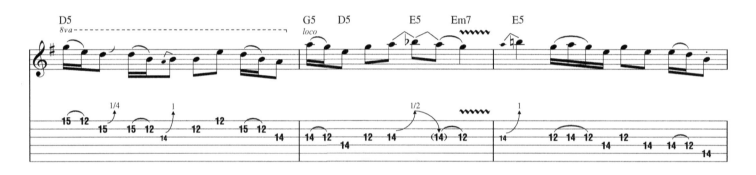

D.S. al Coda

Interlude

Gtrs. 1 & 2: w/ Rhy. Fig. 1 (1st 4 meas., 2 times)
Gtr. 3 tacet

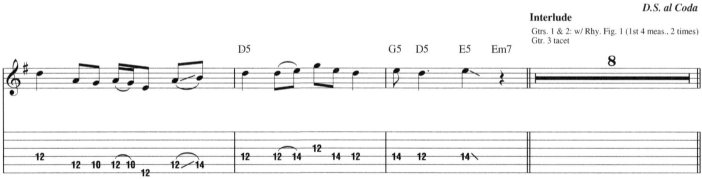

⊕ Coda

Outro

Gtrs. 1 & 2: w/ Rhy. Fig. 1 (1st 7 meas.)

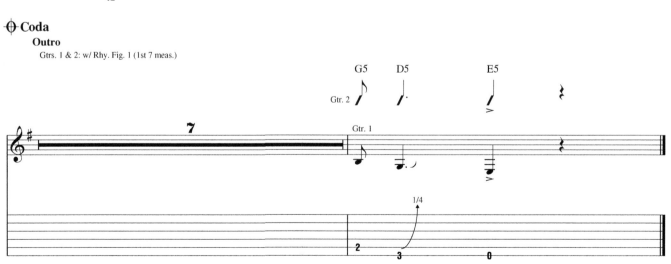

from *Sabbath Bloody Sabbath*

Sabbath, Bloody Sabbath

Words and Music by Frank Iommi, John Osbourne, William Ward and Terence Butler

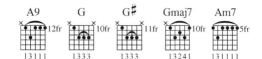

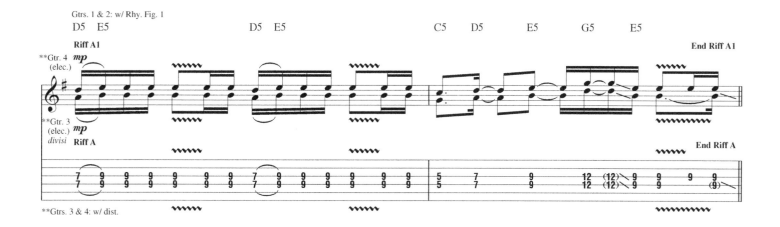

1. You see right through dis-tort-ed eyes,___ you know you have to ___ learn.___

The ex-e-cu-tion of your mind ___ you real-ly have to ___ turn.___

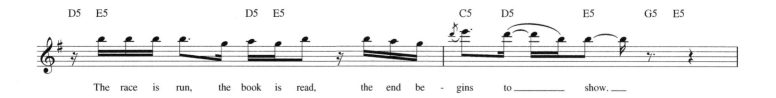

The race is run, the book is read, the end be - gins to _____ show. _____

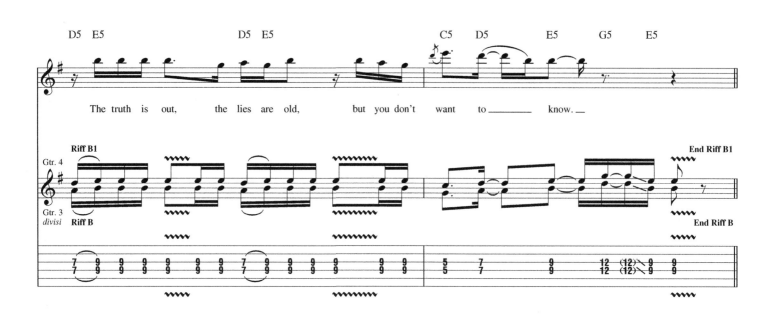

The truth is out, the lies are old, but you don't want to _____ know. _____

Riff B1

Gtr. 4

Gtr. 3
divisi   Riff B

End Riff B1

End Riff B

Chorus

Gtrs. 3 & 4 tacet

Rhy. Fig. 2

*Gtr. 5
(acous.)

A9   G   G#

No - bod - y _____ will ev - er _____ let you _____ know

Gtr. 6 (elec.)

w/ clean tone

Gtr. 7 (elec.)

w/ clean tone

*Two acous. gtrs. arr. for one.

when you ask ___ the rea - sons why. ___

They just tell ___ you that you're on ___ your ___ own,

fill   your   head ____   all ____   full   of ____   lies. _____

Interlude

Gtrs. 1 & 2: w/ Rhy. Fig. 1
Gtrs. 3 & 4: w/ Riffs A & A1
Gtr. 5 tacet

Verse

Gtrs. 1 & 2: w/ Rhy. Fig. 1 (4 times)
Gtrs. 3 & 4: w/ Riffs A & A1 (3 times)

2. The   peo - ple   who   have   crip - pled   you,   you   wan - na   see   them _____   burn. ____

The   gates   of   life   have   closed   on   you   and   there's   just   no   re -   turn. ____

You're   wish - ing   that   the   hands   of   doom   could   take   your   mind   a -   way, ____

Gtrs. 3 & 4: w/ Riffs B & B1

and   you   don't   care   if   you   don't   see   a - gain   the   light   of _____   day. ____

Chorus

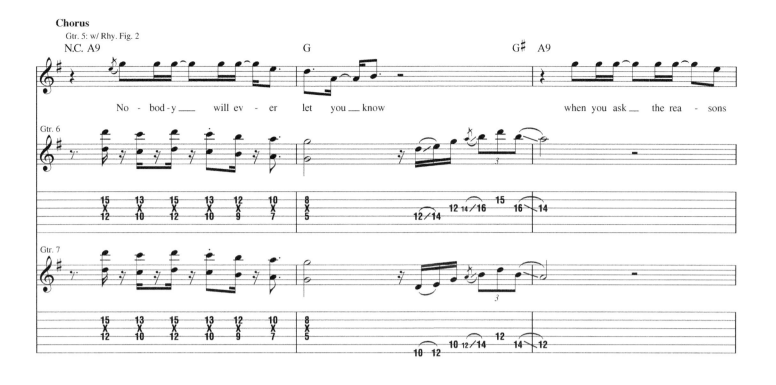

No - bod - y ___ will ev - er __ let you __ know _____ when you ask ___ the rea - sons

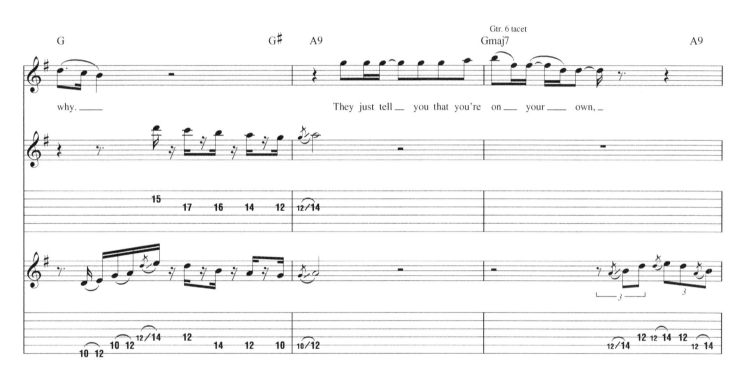

why. ____ They just tell __ you that you're on __ your __ own, __

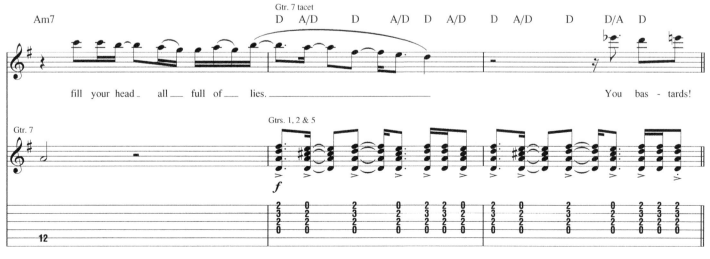

fill your head __ all __ full of __ lies. _____ You bas - tards!

Guitar Solo

Gtrs. 1 & 2: w/ Rhy. Fig. 1 (4 times)
Gtrs. 3 & 4: w/ Riffs A & A1 (4 times)
Gtr. 5 tacet

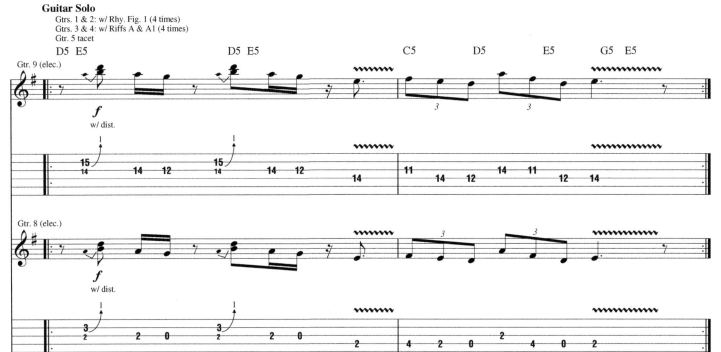

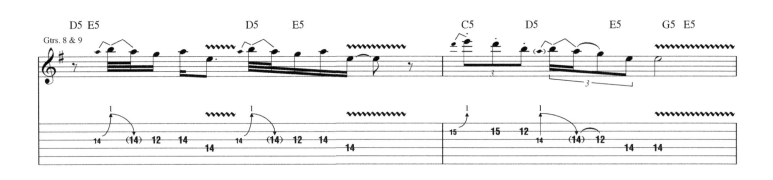

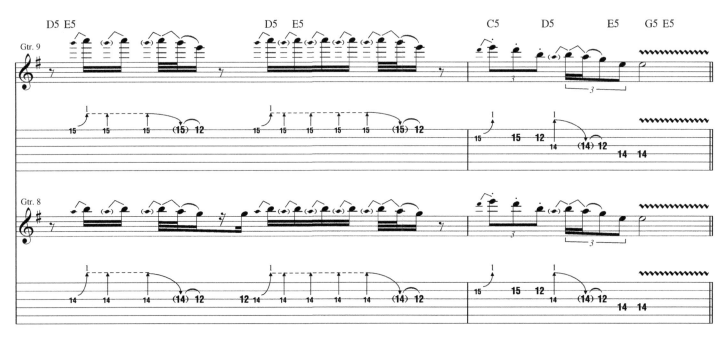

Interlude

Gtrs. 1 & 2: w/ Rhy. Fig. 1
Gtrs. 3 & 4: w/ Riffs B & B1
Gtrs. 8 & 9 tacet

*Chord symbols reflect combined harmony.

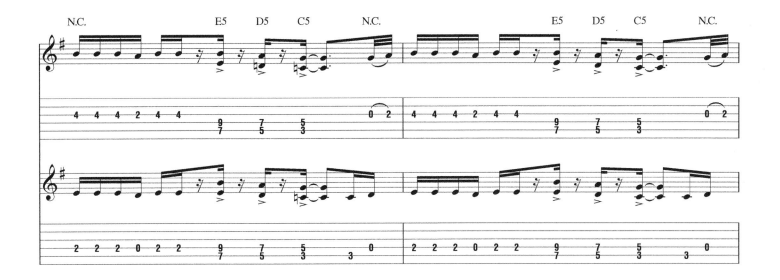

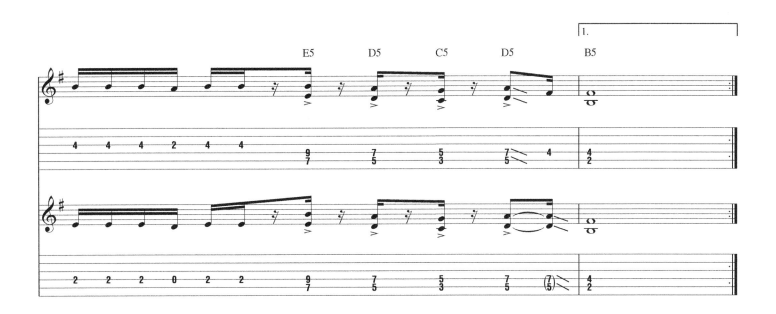

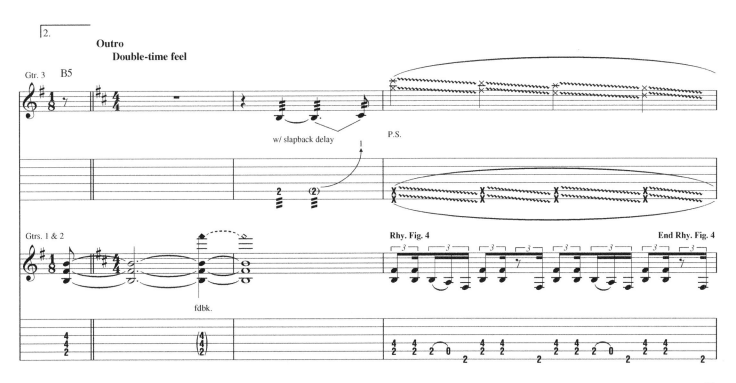

Gtrs. 1 & 2: w/ Rhy. Fig. 4 (till fade)

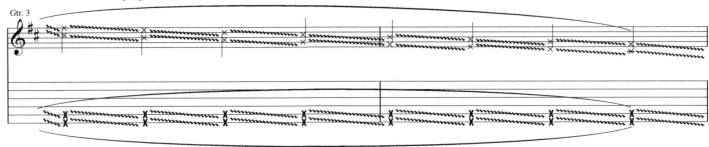

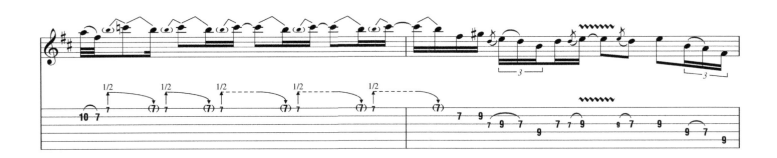

Begin fade

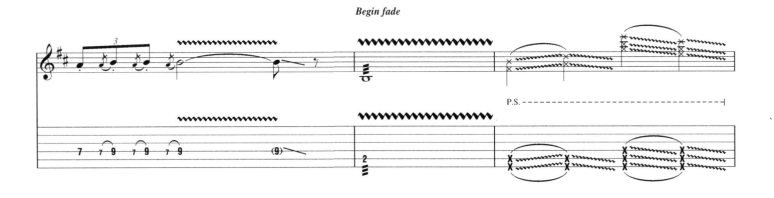

Fade out

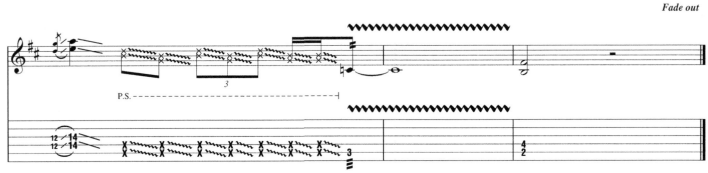

from *Vol. 4*

Supernaut

Words and Music by Frank Iommi, Terence Butler, William Ward and John Osbourne

Tune down 1 1/2 steps:
(low to high) C#-F#-B-E-G#-C#

Intro
Moderately ♩ = 116

*Gtr. 2: w/ wah-wah (used as filter).
Composite arrangement

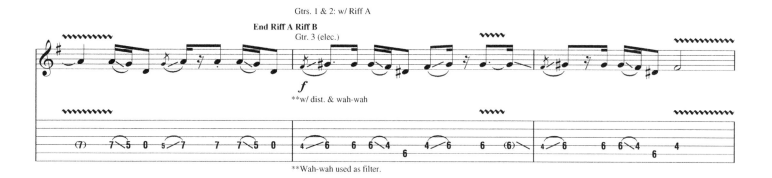

**Wah-wah used as filter.

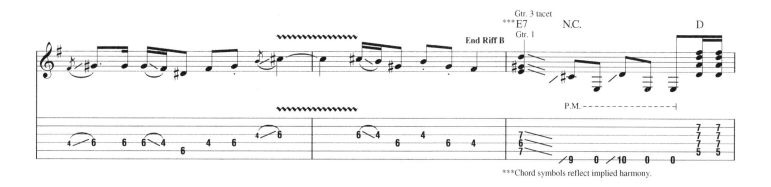

***Chord symbols reflect implied harmony.

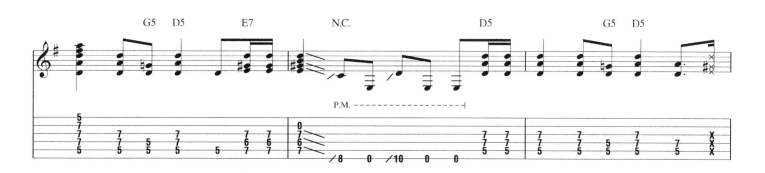

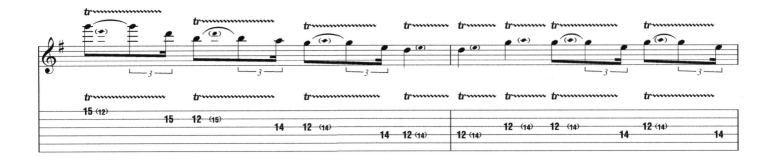

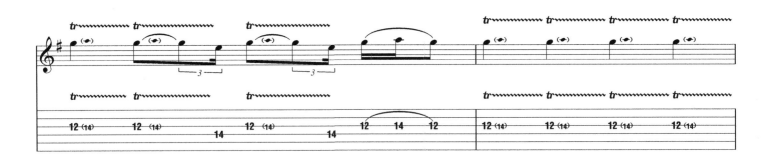

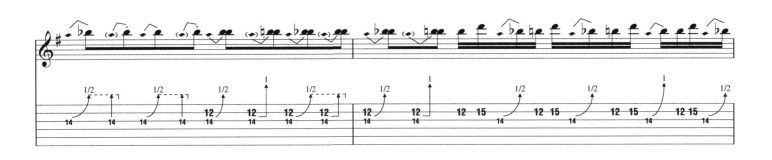

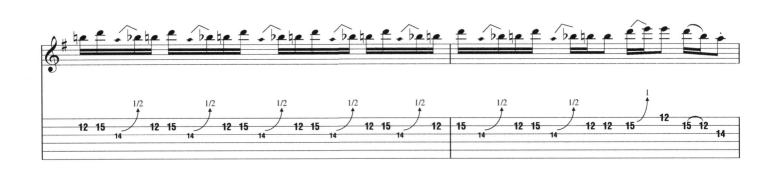

Interlude

Gtrs. 1 & 2: w/ Riff A   Gtr. 4 tacet

N.C.

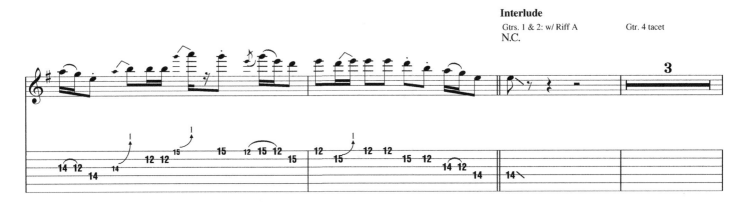

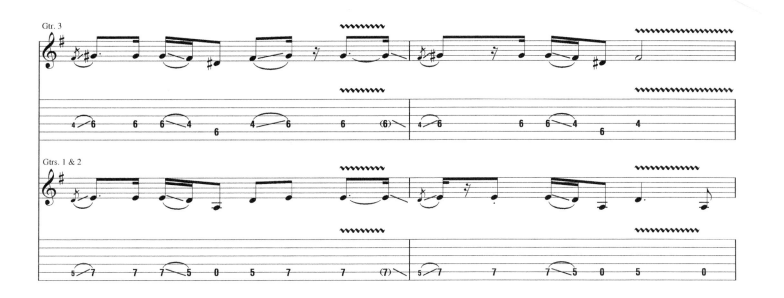

Percussion Solo

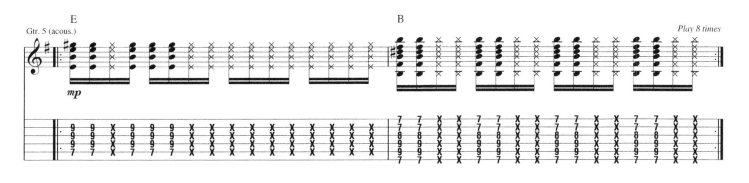

Interlude

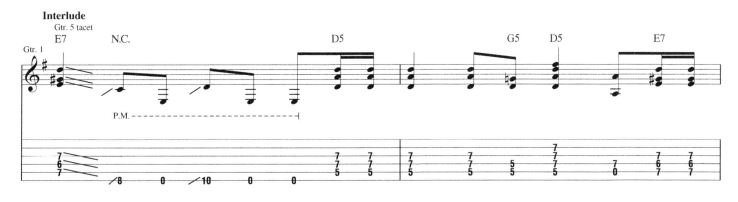

Verse
Gtr. 1: w/ Rhy. Fig. 1 (3 times)

3. Got no re - li - gion, don't need no friends, ___ got all I want and I don't

need to pre - tend. ___ Don't try to reach me, 'cause I'll tear up your mind. ___

Gtr. 1: w/ Rhy. Fig. 2

Outro
Gtrs. 1 & 2: w/ Riff A (till fade)

I've seen the fu - ture and I've left it be - hind. ___

Begin fade   *Fade out*

Gtr. 3: w/ Riff B (till fade)

from *Master of Reality*

Sweet Leaf

Words and Music by Frank Iommi, John Osbourne, William Ward and Terence Butler

from *Sabotage*

Symptom of the Universe

Words and Music by Frank Iommi, John Osbourne, William Ward and Terence Butler

Tune down 1 1/2 steps:
(low to high) C#-F#-B-E-G#-C#

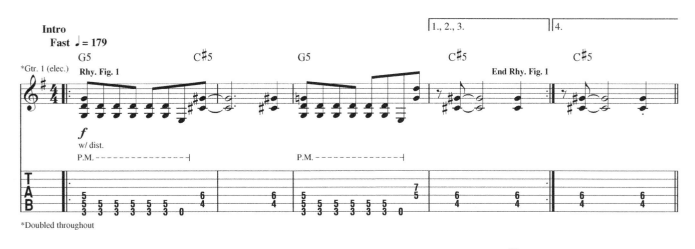

*Doubled throughout

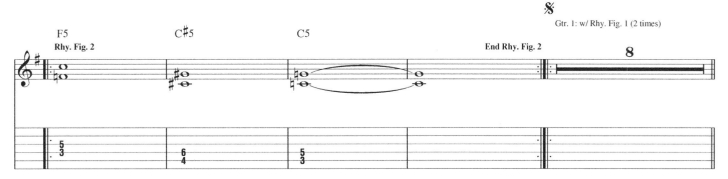

Verse

1. Take me through the cen-tu-ries __ to su-per-son-ic years. _____ E-
2. Moth-er mooch, she's call-ing me __ back to her sil-ver womb. _____
3. Take my hand, my child of love, __ come step in-side my tears. _____

lec-tri-fy-ing en-e-my is drown-ing in his tears. _____
Fath-er of cre-a-tion takes me from my stol-en tomb. _____
Swim the mag-ic o-cean I've __ been cry-ing all __ these years. _____

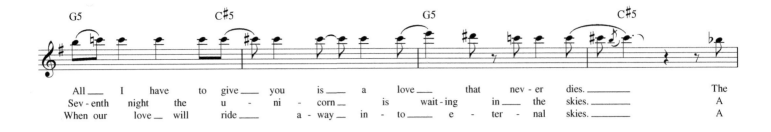

All __ I have to give __ you is __ a love __ that nev - er dies. _____ The
Sev - enth night the u - ni - corn __ is wait - ing in __ the skies. _____ A
When our love __ will ride __ a - way __ in - to __ e - ter - nal skies. _____ A

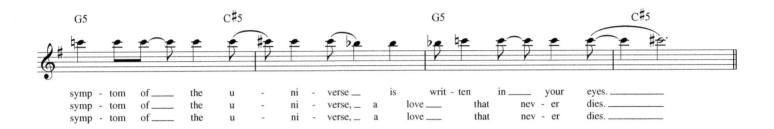

symp - tom of __ the u - ni - verse __ is writ - ten in __ your eyes. _____
symp - tom of __ the u - ni - verse, __ a love __ that nev - er dies. _____
symp - tom of __ the u - ni - verse, __ a love __ that nev - er dies. _____

Interlude

Gtr. 1: w/ Rhy. Fig. 2 (2 times)

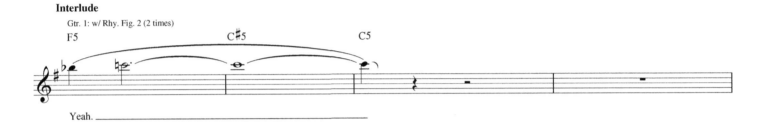

Yeah. _____

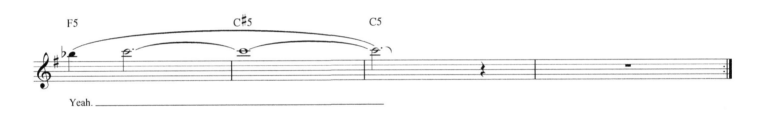

Yeah. _____

1. - 7.   8.   *To Coda*   **D.S. al Coda**

Interlude

Gtr. 1: w/ Rhy. Fig. 2 (2 times)

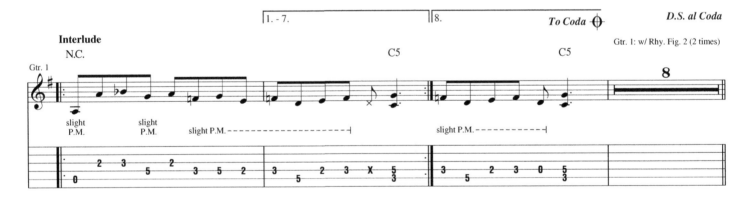

Coda

Slower ♩ = 171

*D5

*Chord symbols reflect implied harmony.

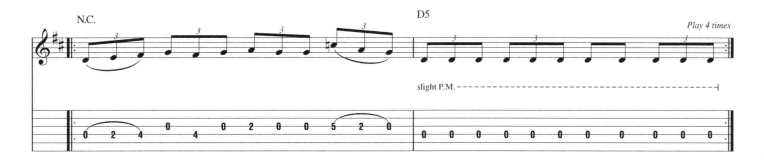

Guitar Solo

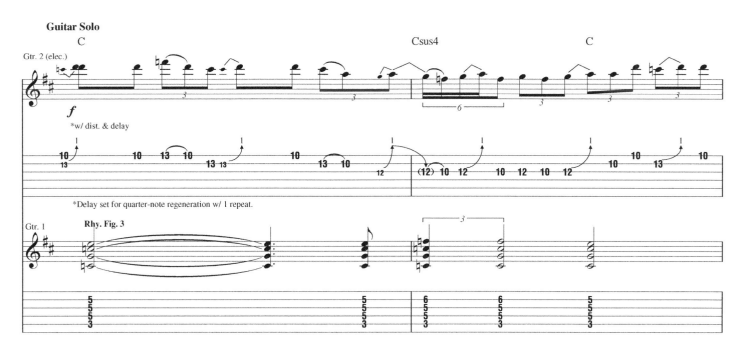

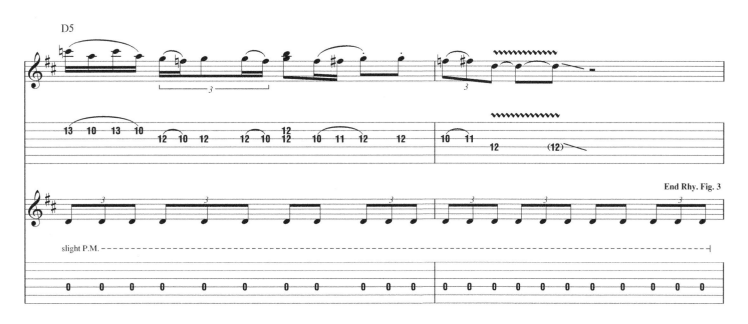

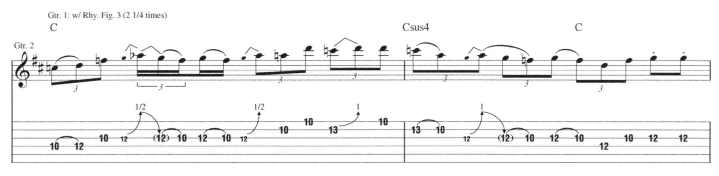

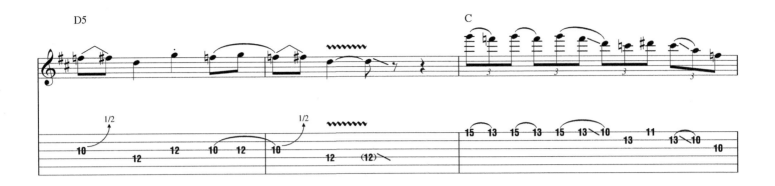

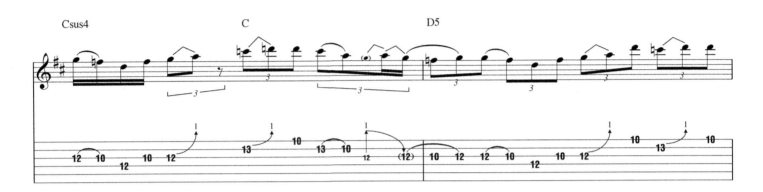

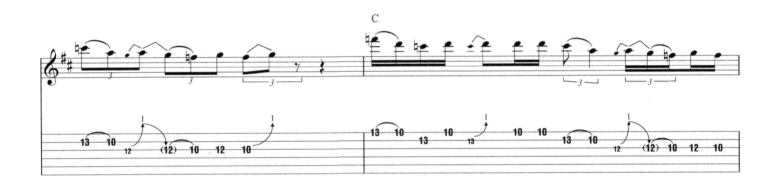

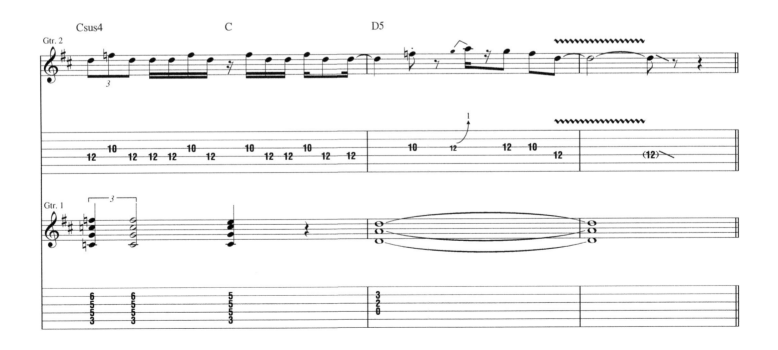

Interlude
Much slower ♩ = 86 (♫ = ♫)

Gtr. 2 tacet

| D5/A | D#5/A# | E5/B | F5/C | F#5/C# | G5/D | G#5/D# | A5/E |

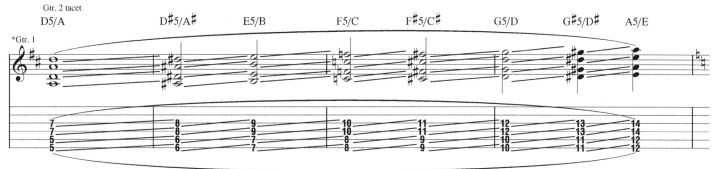

*Simulated tape effect in which tape speed
 is gradually increased to raise pitch 3 1/2 steps.

Gtr.1 tacet

| Am | D7sus4 | D | Am | D7sus4 | D |

Gtr. 4 (acous.)

mf

Riff A
*Gtr. 3 (acous.)

mf

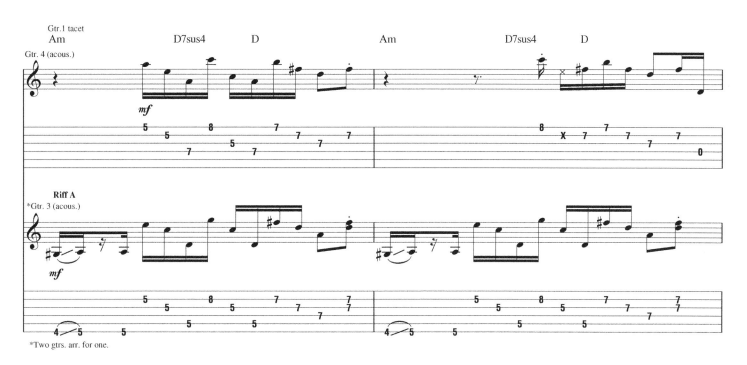

*Two gtrs. arr. for one.

Gtr. 4 tacet

| Am | D7sus4 | D | Am | D7sus4 | D |

Gtr. 3

Wom - an, child ____

End Riff A

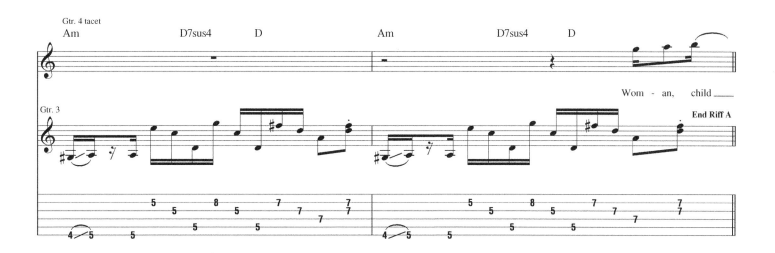

Bridge

Gtr. 3: w/ Riff A (4 times)

| Am | D7sus4 | D | Am | D7sus4 | D |

____ of love's cre - a - tion, _____ come and step ____ in - side ____ my

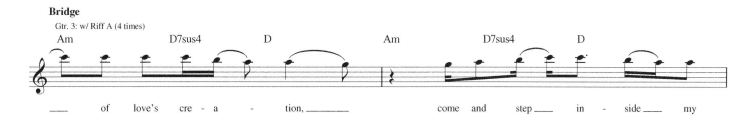

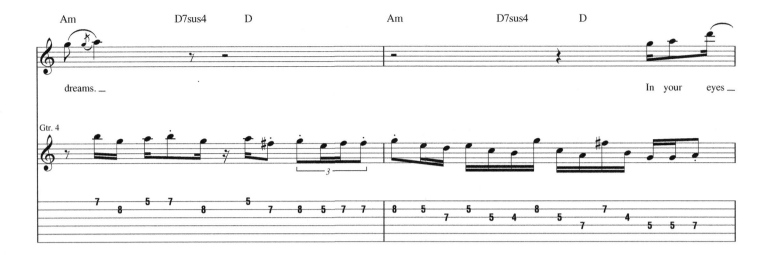

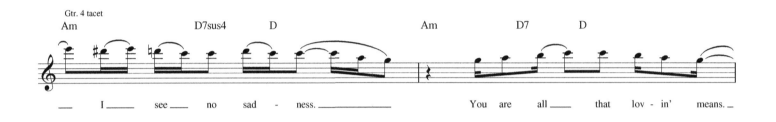

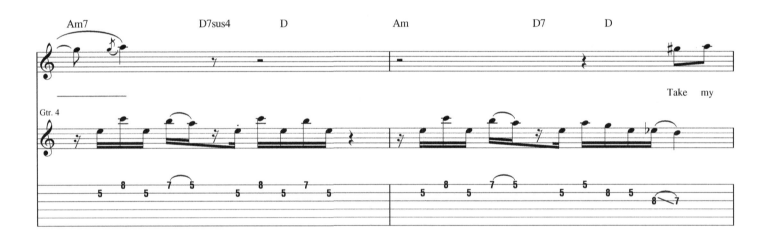

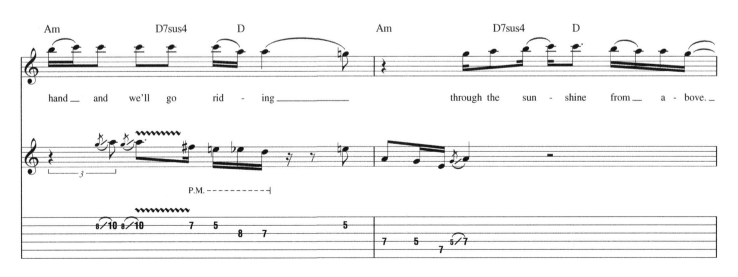

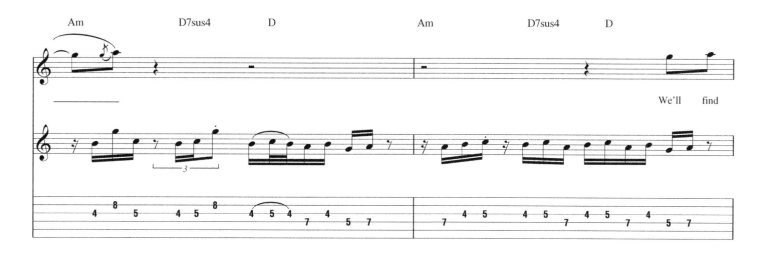

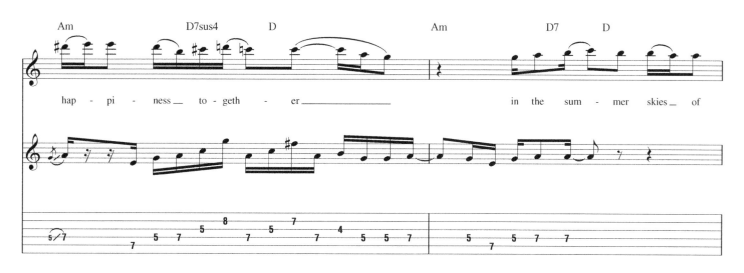

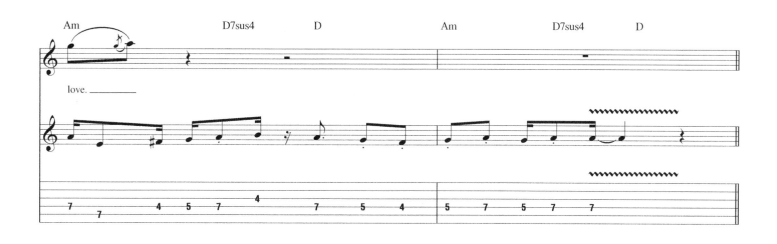

Outro-Guitar Solo

Gtr. 3: w/ Riff A (till fade)

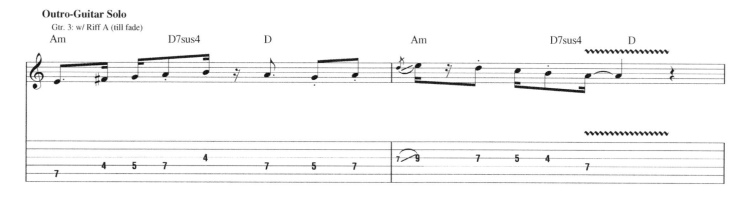

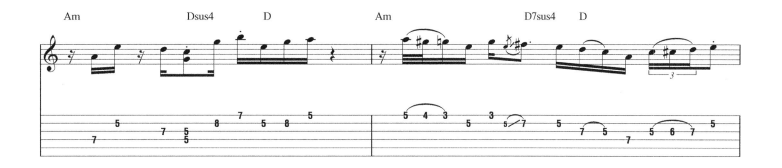

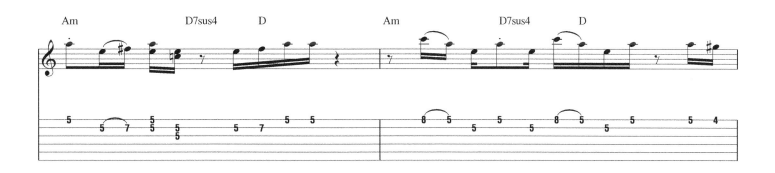

Begin fade

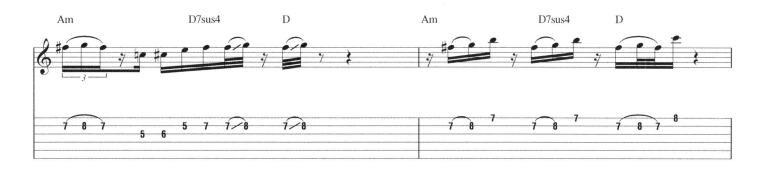

Fade out

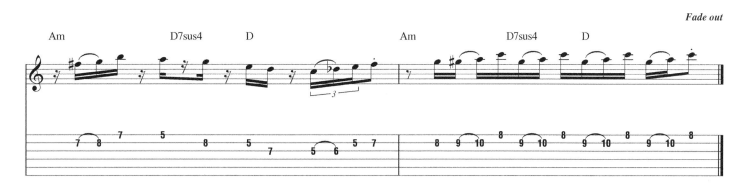

from *The Mob Rules*

Voodoo

Words by Ronnie James Dio
Music by Ronnie James Dio, Terence Butler and Anthony Iommi

Tune down 1/2 step:
(low to high) Eb-Ab-Db-Gb-Bb-Eb

Intro
Moderately ♩ = 102

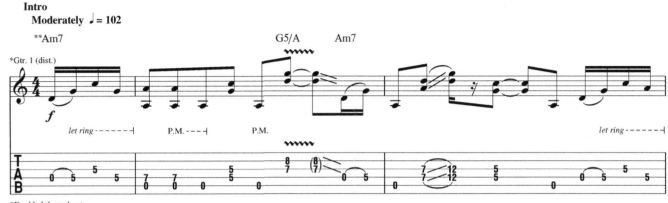

*Gtr. 1 (dist.)

*Doubled throughout
 **Chord symbols reflect implied harmony.

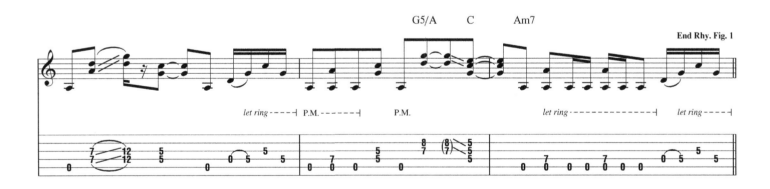

Verse
Gtr. 1: w/ Rhy. Fig. 1 (1 1/2 times)

1. Say you don't love me, you'll burn. ____ You can re- fuse, ____ but you'll lose, ____

it's by me. Say you don't want me, you'll learn. ____

Noth - ing you do will be new, ____ 'cause I'm through. Oh. ____

Rhy. Fig. 2

Gtr. 1

P.M. ----------

End Rhy. Fig. 2

Interlude

Gtr. 1: w/ Rhy. Fig. 1

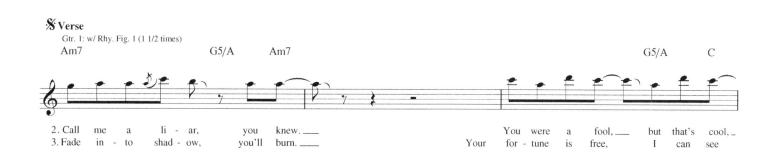

Verse

Gtr. 1: w/ Rhy. Fig. 1 (1 1/2 times)

2. Call me a li - ar, you knew. ____ You were a fool, ____ but that's cool, ____
3. Fade in - to shad - ow, you'll burn. ____ Your for - tune is free, I can see

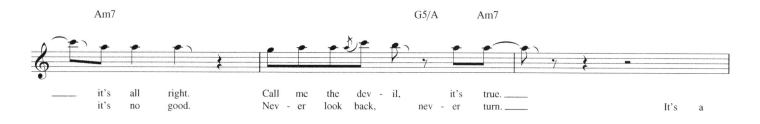

____ it's all right. Call me the dev - il, it's true. ____
it's no good. Nev - er look back, nev - er turn. ____ It's a

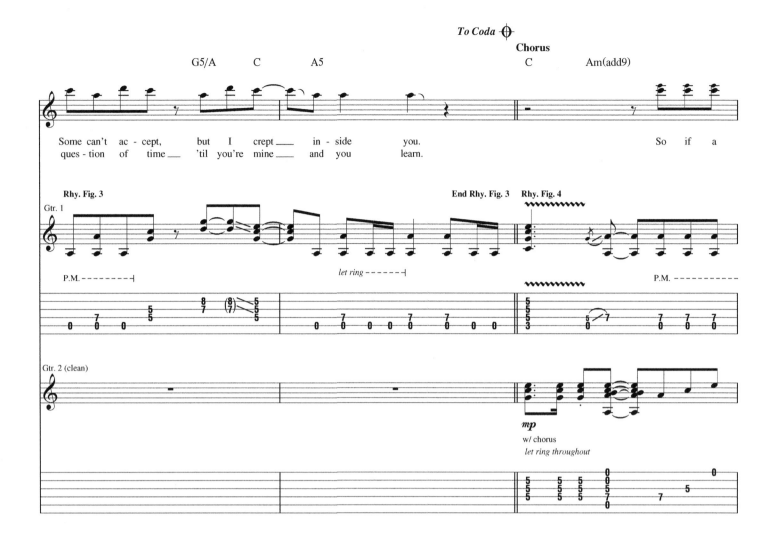

Some can't ac - cept, but I crept ___ in - side you. So if a
ques - tion of time ___ 'til you're mine ___ and you learn.

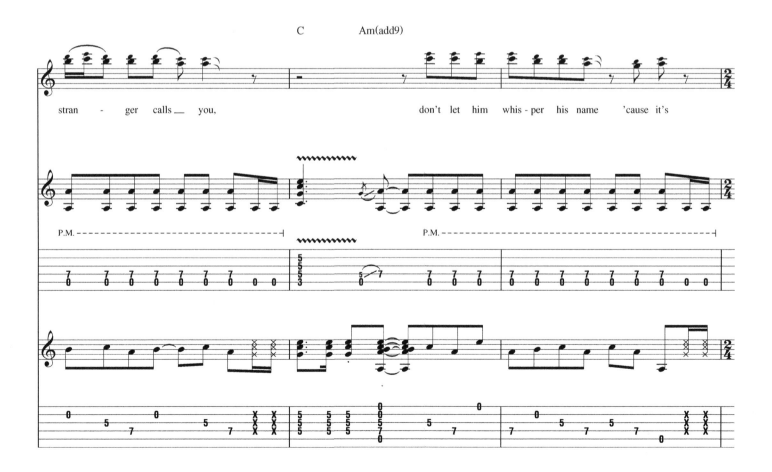

stran - ger calls ___ you, don't let him whis - per his name 'cause it's

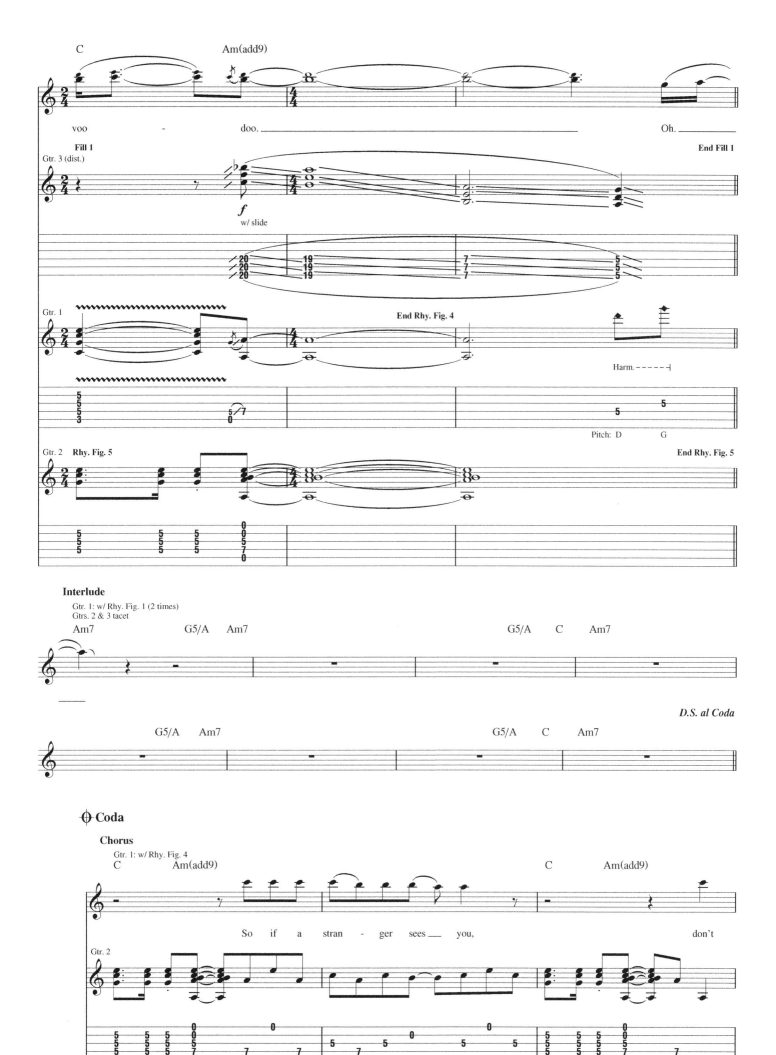

look in his eyes 'cause he's   voo -   doo.

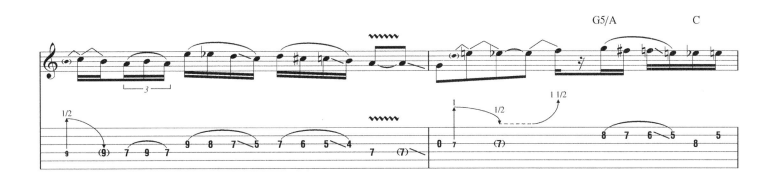

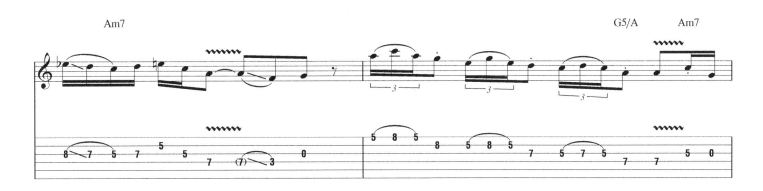

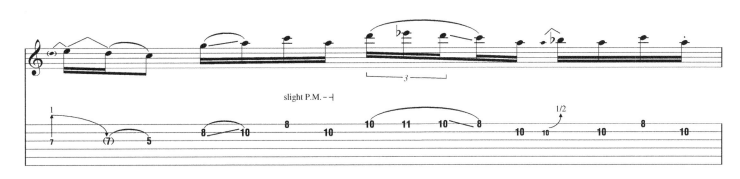

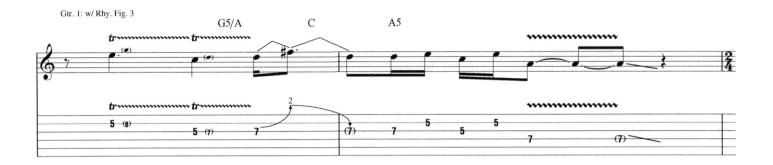

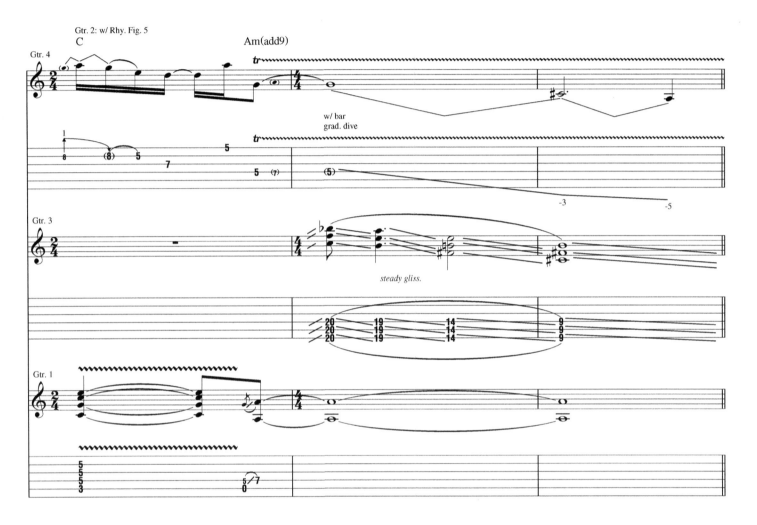

Verse

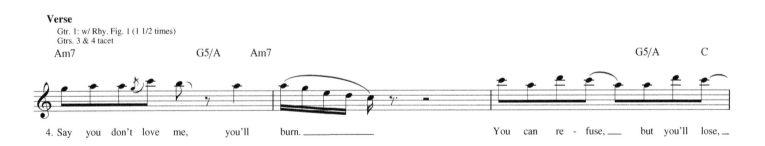

4. Say you don't love me, you'll burn._____ You can re - fuse,___ but you'll lose,___

____ it's by me. Say you don't want me, you'll learn.___

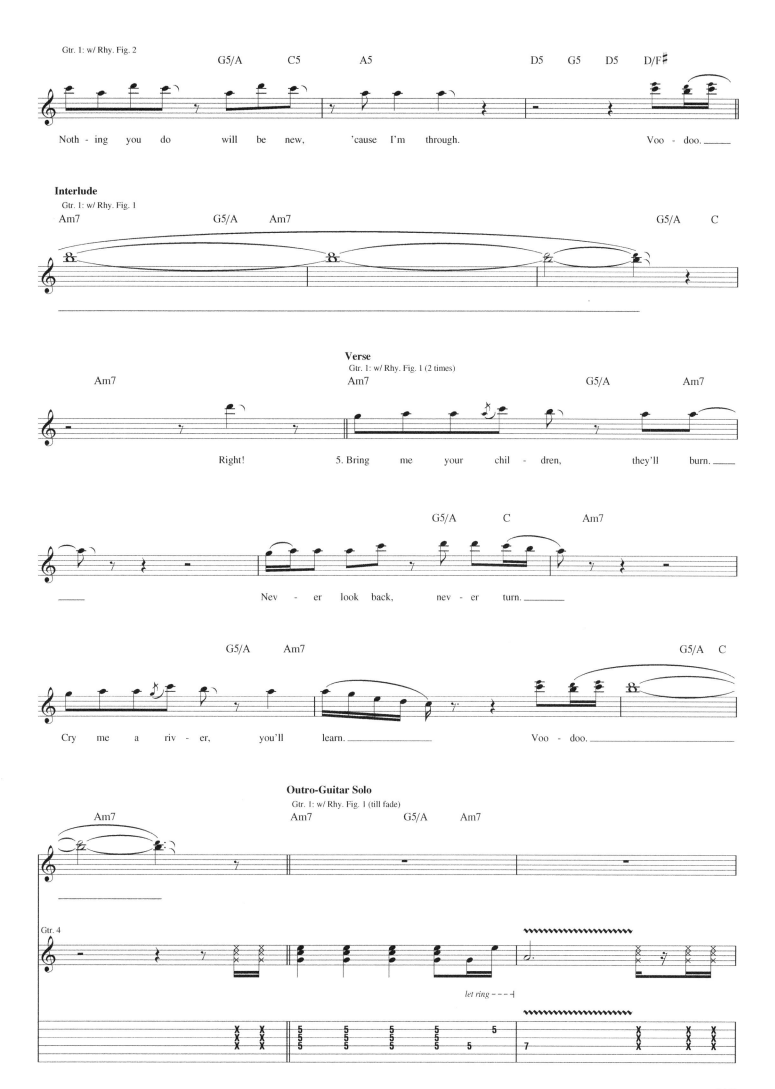

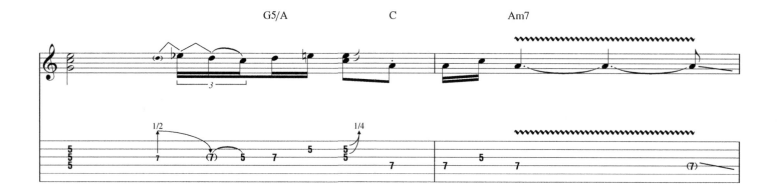

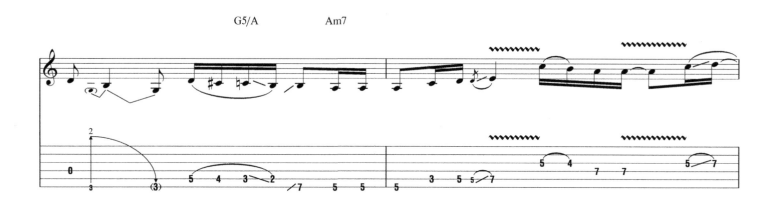

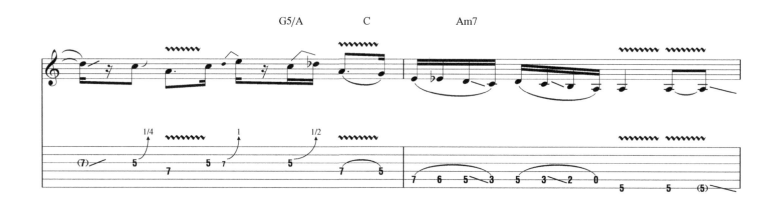

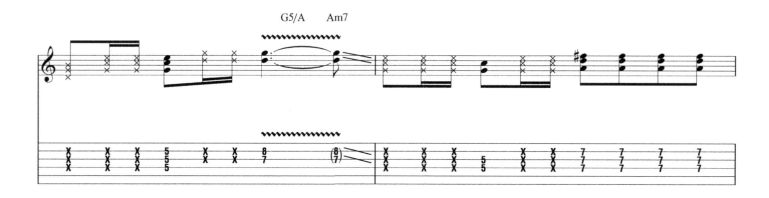

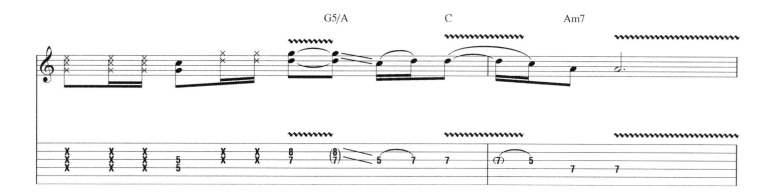

Begin fade

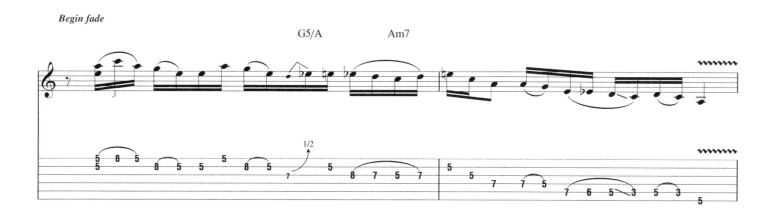

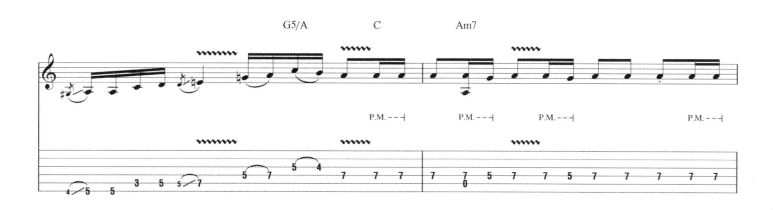

Fade out

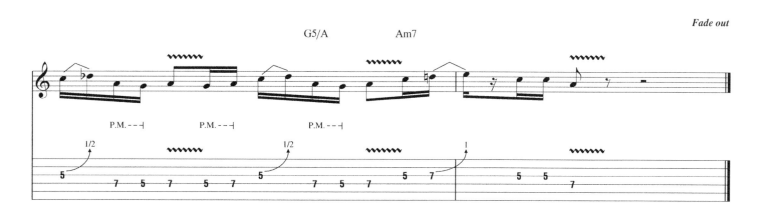

War Pigs (Interpolating Luke's Wall)

Words and Music by Frank Iommi, John Osbourne, William Ward and Terence Butler

Preamble
Slowly ♩. = 56

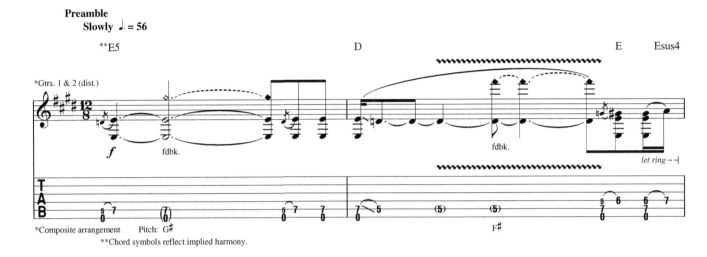

*Composite arrangement   Pitch: G♯

**Chord symbols reflect implied harmony.

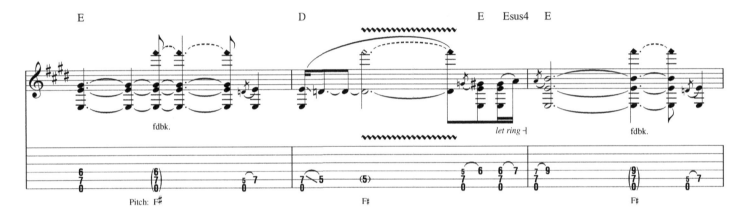

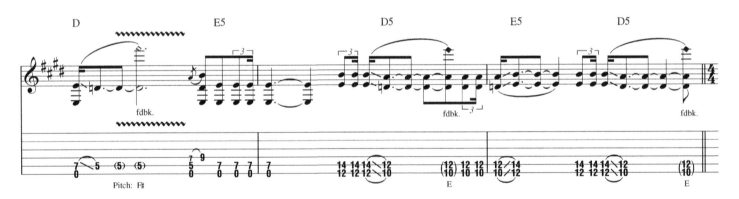

% Intro
Faster ♩ = 88

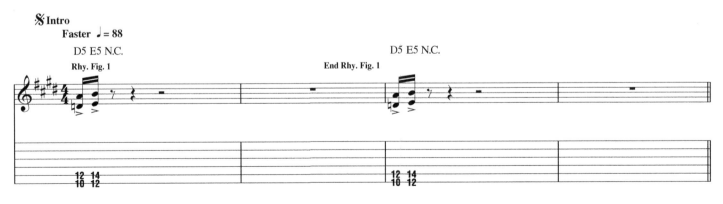

Why should they _ go out _ to _____ fight? _ They leave that _ role to the _ poor! _____ Yeah!
Treat - ing peo - ple just like pawns in _ chess, _ wail 'til their Judge - ment Day _ comes. _____ Yeah!

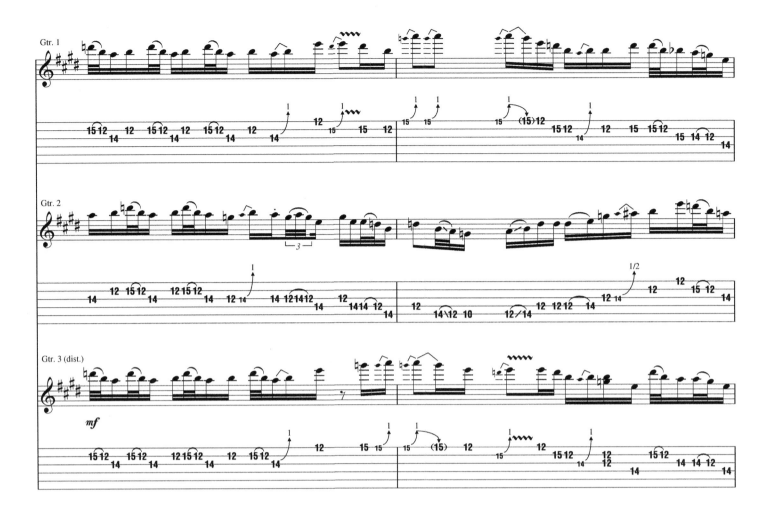

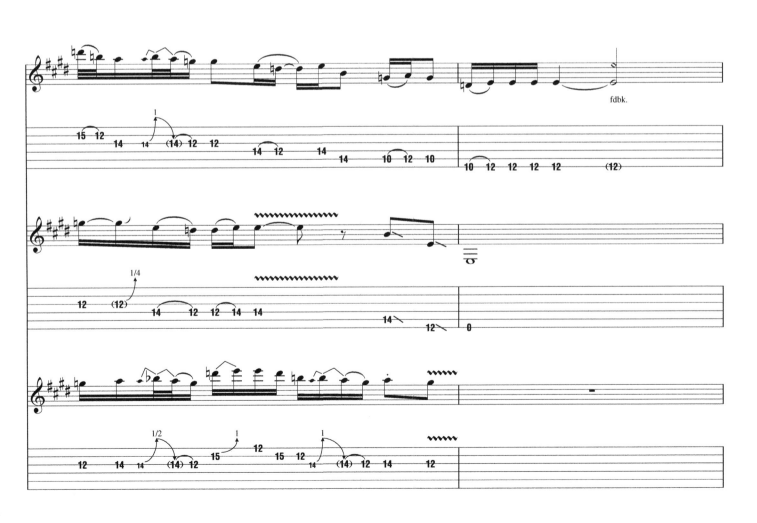

*Gtrs. 1 & 2
Gtr. 3 tacet

*Composite arrangement

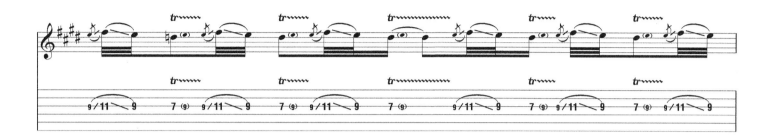

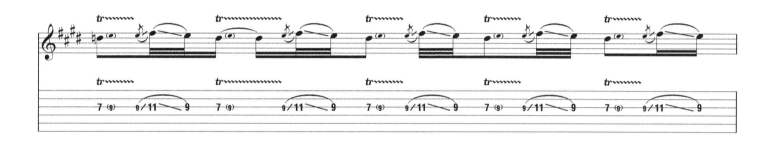

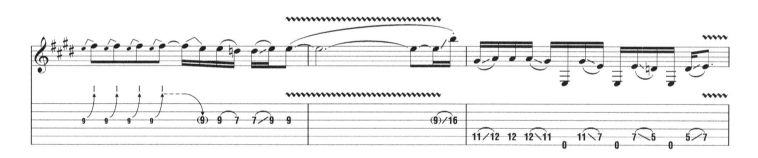

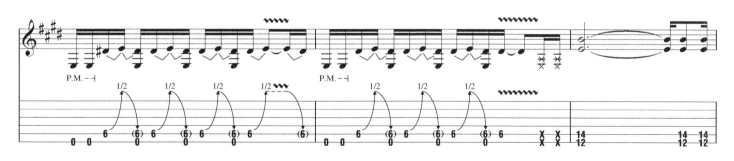

D.S. al Coda
(take repeat)

D5

E5

D5

fdbk.

Pitch: E

*Studio effect: tape speeds up gradually until chord sounds 10 1/2 steps higher.